Applied Economics and Policy Studies

The Applied Economics and Policy Studies present latest theoretical and methodological discussions to bear on the scholarly works covering economic theories, econometric analyses, as well as multifaceted issues arising out of emerging concerns from different industries and debates surrounding latest policies. Situated at the forefront of the interdisciplinary fields of applied economics and policy studies, this book series seeks to bring together the scholarly insights centering on economic development, infrastructure development, macroeconomic policy, governance of welfare policy, policies and governance of emerging markets, and relevant subfields that trace to the discipline of applied economics, public policy, policy studies, and combined fields of the aforementioned. The book series of Applied Economics and Policy Studies is dedicated to the gathering of intellectual views by scholars and policymakers. The publications included are relevant for scholars, policymakers, and students of economics, policy studies, and otherwise interdisciplinary programs.

More information about this series at https://link.springer.com/bookseries/16776

Xiaolong Li · Jiyin Li · Chunhui Yuan ·
Songliang Guo · Zhen Wang

Development Practice of Digital Business Environment in China

Springer

Xiaolong Li
Department of Postal Management
Beijing University of Posts
and Telecommunications
Beijing, China

Jiyin Li
Information Center of Ministry of Industry
and Information Technology
Beijing, China

Chunhui Yuan
School of Economics and Management
Beijing University of Posts
and Telecommunications
Beijing, China

Songliang Guo
School of Economics and Management
Beijing University of Posts
and Telecommunications
Beijing, China

Zhen Wang
School of Economics and Management
Beijing University of Posts
and Telecommunications
Beijing, China

ISSN 2731-4006 ISSN 2731-4014 (electronic)
Applied Economics and Policy Studies
ISBN 978-981-16-8526-2 ISBN 978-981-16-8527-9 (eBook)
https://doi.org/10.1007/978-981-16-8527-9

This Springer imprint is published by the registered company Springer Nature Singapore Pte Ltd.
The registered company address is: 152 Beach Road, #21-01/04 Gateway East, Singapore 189721, Singapore

Contents

Chapter 1
Introduction

Abstract Digital technology is the new engine of industrial development during the new industrial revolution, and it is the main driving force for the formation and development of digital economy. Digital technology in a narrow sense mainly refers to the technology of coding, computing, processing, storing, transmitting, spreading, restoring and applying numbers. In recent years, the global digital economy has grown vigorously, which has provided countries with effective channels to create new economic growth points and new economic drivers. Countries have seized development opportunities in an attempt to seize or lock-in more digital economic development dividends. Since the outbreak of the Covid-19, Chinese online economy has taken the lead in the world. Epidemic has intensified the competition between countries for development dividends, and the digital business environment has become the focus of global competition in the 'post-epidemic era', which aims to build a data transaction platform and ensure data security.

1.1 Digital Technology Iterative Innovation Brings About the Transformation of Business

Digital technology is the new engine of industrial development during the new industrial revolution, and it is the main driving force for the formation and development of digital economy. Digital technology in a narrow sense mainly refers to the technology of coding, computing, processing, storing, transmitting, spreading, restoring and applying numbers. Digital technology in a broad sense includes binary coding digital technology, 5G communication artificial intelligence, blockchain, big data, cloud computing, internet of things, advanced robot additive manufacturing (3D printing), virtual reality technology, etc. With the continuous reform and innovation of digital technology, the production factor system has been reconstructed. The integration and innovation of digital technology and other fields have been accelerated. New application models have broken through. Traditional industries have been transformed into digitalization. New formats and new models have matured. The platform economy has been developed, and the business environment has gradually

X. Li et al., *Development Practice of Digital Business Environment in China*, Applied Economics and Policy Studies,
https://doi.org/10.1007/978-981-16-8527-9_1

changed. Traditional market transactions mainly focus on three factors of production: labor, land and capital. With the application innovation of digital technology, data has become one of the most dynamic factors of production in the market. As a new factor of production in digital economy, the marketization and value characteristics of data will become increasingly obvious. By the end of 2020, the scale of data generated in the world will exceed 50ZB. The huge amount of data drives the traditional business around land, labor and capital to extend to the digital business environment of building a data trading platform and ensuring data security.

During the period of the 13th five-year plan, the average annual growth rate of massive data in China exceeded 50%, accounting for 20% in the world, making it one of the countries with the largest amount of data and the richest types of data. On April 9, 2020, the Opinions of the Central Committee of the Communist Party of China and the State Council on Constructing a Better System and Mechanism of Factor Marketization Allocation was officially promulgated, which listed data, land, labor, capital and technology as production factors for the first time, aiming at deepening the market-oriented reform of factor allocation and promoting the quality, efficiency and power changes of economic development. During the period of the 14th Five-Year Plan, the market-oriented reform of data elements will continue to be further promoted. China will further improve the circulation efficiency and market vitality of data elements from the aspects of promoting the open sharing of government data, enhancing the value of social data resources, strengthening the integration and security protection of data resources, etc. They will give full play to the multiplier effect of data as a new element on the efficiency of traditional elements, so that data elements will become a new kinetic energy to promote the high-quality development of digital economy. Digital technology and other fields will accelerate integration and innovation, and new application modes will break through development. The integration of digital technology with biological sciences, new materials, energy, transportation and other fields has created new industrial forms and business models such as industrial Internet, energy Internet, intelligent materials and biochips, and triggered a multi-field, multi-dimensional, systematic and revolutionary group breakthrough. Lightweight and intelligence have become the development trend of new material technology, and new material technology is accelerating its development towards intelligence. In 2020, intelligent materials technologies such as self-repairing materials, adaptive materials, new sensing materials and 4D printing materials will emerge in large numbers, providing support for the development of biomedical, aerospace and other fields. The United States, Japan, South Korea and other countries have accelerated breakthroughs in new material technologies such as graphene devices, additive manufacturing processes, nanoparticle processing and biomaterial preparation. For example, South Korea's Implementation Plan for Technology Development in Nanomaterials Field in 2019 aims to systematically support the development of core technologies of future new semiconductor devices with human brain computing capabilities and study future materials with new features and functions.

Digital technology has continuously driven the products or services of traditional industries to be digitized and intelligent. The management mode has made a breakthrough in the direction of flattening management, and the operating efficiency has been continuously improved. WEF pointed out that digital transformation can help reduce the cost of the manufacturing industry by about 17.6% and help the manufacturing industry to increase operating income by about 22.6%.[1] Meanwhile, digital transformation and upgrading can also have favored logistics industry. Specifically, it can help the logistics industry reduce the cost by about 34.2% and increase the operating income by about 33.6%.

Manufacturing is becoming an important field in the application scenario of digital economy. During the period of 13th five-year plan, China's digital economy and the real economy accelerated integration. As the main battlefield of the real economy, the digital transformation of manufacturing industry was further promoted, which became the consensus of all kinds of manufacturing enterprises to build new market competitiveness. The "14th Five-Year Plan" period is a key stage for China to realize the transformation from a big manufacturing country to a powerful manufacturing country. Digital transformation will be an important force to promote the high-quality development of manufacturing with intelligent manufacturing as the main direction, and digital application scenarios will be used more and more in the manufacturing field. In terms of manufacturing hardware, the intelligent transformation of the whole production cycle will become the focus, and industrial robots, intelligent production lines and unmanned factories will be further promoted to minimize manual intervention. They will improve the overall cooperation efficiency of production facilities, and improve product quality consistency. In terms of manufacturing software, technologies such as cloud computing, big data, and artificial intelligence will be integrated and applied in the whole process of manufacturing, operation and management, and sales services. They will accelerate personalized customization, network collaborative manufacturing, and remote operation and maintenance services. The formation of intelligent manufacturing models. In terms of manufacturing ecology, collaborative innovation will be continuously strengthened among intelligent equipment manufacturing, logistics and warehousing, and software professional enterprises to strengthen the supply capacity of system solutions. The ecosystem of manufacturing integration and development will become the mainstream of industrial chain supply chain stability and competitiveness improvement.

At the same time, the vigorous development of information technologies such as the Internet, artificial intelligence, cloud computing and big data has not only brought great changes to human society, but also promoted the digital transformation of traditional enterprises. Government departments are also using information technology to deeply adjust their organizational structure and business processes, promote the migration of government offline business to online digital space, shorten the distance between people and accelerate the digital transformation of government. The United States has explored and tried the business collaboration, management standards and procurement mode of digital government. The Government Transformation Strategy (2017–2020) issued by the United Kingdom in 2017 aims to achieve cross-departmental business integration and flexible working methods, improve the

[1] Data Source: The World Economic Forum. The Impact of the Fourth Industrial Revolution on Supply Chain.

government's digital skills, and make better use of data. Singapore adheres to the concept of "governing the country with big data" and uses big data analysis to accurately predict citizens' needs and optimize the purpose of public service supply. The electronic driver's license launched by South Korea, the virtual business trip in Japan, the digital medical care in the UK, etc. Our country also launched the application like 12,123, the Government Online Service Hall, the QR code for epidemic prevention and control, *Health* Pal, etc. Compared with disadvantages of traditional government service activities with redundant processes, alienating from the masses, and paper-based office operation, these new processing methods not only improve the work efficiency and advance a deeper reform in the system of administrative and approval, but also provide enterprise with great convenience. The Digital-Business environment is unceasingly optimized on its way. In order to speed up the construction of digital government, local governments in China have successively set up government service and big data management agencies to introduce the plan of digital government. On October 8, 2019, the State Council promulgated the Regulations on Optimizing Business Environment, which put forward higher requirements for protecting market players, creating a fair competitive market environment, optimizing government services, implementing supervision and law enforcement, and strengthening legal protection. Optimizing the business environment is an important indicator for evaluating the effectiveness of government digital transformation, which is a key factor for the success of optimizing the business environment. Moreover, the iterative innovation of digital technology has also improved the efficiency of production and resource allocation, and more importantly, it is changing people's lifestyles and social business models. In the traditional business credit model, information asymmetry is the norm. Trust needs to be accumulated, and it takes a long period to establish credit. Trust needs a central node, and daily economic behavior is difficult to become a social credit record. Therefore, the credit accessibility and coverage are small, and the cost of credit formation and credit risk is high. Big data discovers credit and discovers credit value through data mining. Blockchain solves the trust problem by mathematical methods, and expresses rules by algorithmic programs. As long as the common algorithmic programs are trusted, mutual trust can be established, and a trust mechanism of "technical endorsement" can be constructed. Its value lies in that it can form a trustworthy bond in an environment where trust is unknown or weak, thus saving the time and cost needed for credit formation. Digital trust can replace commercial credit to a certain extent, and can bless commercial credit.

With the iterative innovation of digital technologies such as artificial intelligence, big data, 5G, and Internet of Things, the industries penetrated by unmanned applications and online services will be further expanded, and the sparks of new formats and modes generated by the collision between traditional industries. Intelligent technologies will continue to emerge, bringing consumers smarter interactive terminals, richer content resources, and more interesting scene experiences, and providing producers with smarter production decisions, more accurate process control, and lower labor and resource costs. In 2020, the epidemic caused long-term isolation at home and social alienation, which triggered a new mechanism for the digital survival of the whole people. On the demand side, the full combination of big data and artificial intelligence has given intelligent terminals more real-time and accurate service capabilities. People are increasingly accustomed to spending, entertaining and socializing in digital space. New business models such as online education, Internet medical care, telecommuting and live delivery have created more and more new demands for digital consumption. On the supply side, online services have expanded from the low value-added links of "single service on demand" such as housekeeping, take-out, express delivery and housing agency to the high value-added links of "diversified supply of scene-based services" such as education, medical care, office and entertainment. The "unmanned economy", represented by unmanned factories, unmanned warehouses, unmanned patrol, unmanned distribution, unmanned supermarkets, etc., has made great strides in production, logistics, retail, entertainment and other fields, leading production and consumption to a new stage of data intelligence and man–machine collaboration.[2]

In addition, digital technology is also the foundation of platform economy, and its iterative innovation provides the core power for the development of platform economy. The rapid development and application of digital technology is the decisive factor on the supply side of platform economic development. Without the development and application of digital technology, the platform economy will lose its vitality. These technologies include, but are not limited to, computing technology, communication network technology, information processing technology, electronic payment technology, network security technology, Internet of Things, artificial intelligence, 5G, virtual reality, blockchain technology and so on. The driving role of digital technology in the development of platform economy is obvious. As of December 2020, the number of mobile Internet users in China reached 989 million, nearly 1 billion. The proportion of netizens using mobile phones to access the Internet is 99.7%. The number of online shopping users reached 782 million, accounting for 79.1% of the total netizens. The number of online video users reached 927 million, accounting for 93.7% of the total netizens. The number of online payment users reached 854 million, accounting for 86.4% of the total netizens. The number of online education users reached 342 million, accounting for 34.6% of the total netizens. The number of online medical users reached 215 million, accounting for 21.7% of the total netizens. The number of telecommuting users reached 346 million, accounting for 34.9% of the total netizens. Deloitte Research Institute predicts that by 2030, the platform economy will create 77 trillion −110 trillion yuan of tax sources for China.[3]

In addition, digital technology is also the foundation of platform economy, and the iterative innovation of technologies provides the core power for the growth of platform economy. Generally speaking, infrastructure in traditional business environment more often refers to land, buildings, water and electricity, etc., while infrastructure in digital business environment refers more often to new infrastructure such as network infrastructure and modern logistics transportation and so on. In terms of network infrastructure, the iterative innovation of digital technology, especially the application of 5G technology, has driven the development of many industries. The data shows that the popularization and application of 5G technology will drive about

1.8 trillion communication data traffic purchases in the next five years,[2] driving about 4.3 trillion yuan of terminal product purchases and about 2 trillion yuan of data service purchases,[3] contributing to China's digital economy close to 15.2 trillion yuan. In modern logistics and transportation field, the emergence of automated logistics, unmanned aerial vehicles, high-precision maps, and cold chain transportation technologies provide the conditions for the incubation of new business models to pass through the space and time barrier. For example, Cainiao's Courier Station is applying to the Internet of Things (IoT) strategy, who uses digital technologies such as AGV, autonomous driving and AI voice assistant in enterprise business, which leads the logistics industry to make great strides towards AI area.[4]

1.2 The Vigorous Global Digital Economy Provides a Solid Foundation for Digital Business Environment

In recent years, the global digital economy has grown vigorously, which has provided countries with effective channels to create new economic growth points and new economic drivers. Countries have seized development opportunities in an attempt to seize or lock-in more digital economic development dividends. Since the outbreak of the Covid-19, Chinese online economy has taken the lead in the world. Epidemic has intensified the competition between countries for development dividends, and the digital business environment has become the focus of global competition in the "post-epidemic era."

The world is currently undergoing an unprecedented change in a century. Along with the outbreak of Covid-19, the rampant virus has a profound impact on the international status of all countries and increased their instability dramatically compared with the previous ones. Globally, as of 2019, in 47 economies, the added value of digital economy reached 31.8 trillion US dollars, up 1.6 trillion US dollars compared with last year. The digital economy accounted for 41.5% of GDP, up 1.2 percentage points compared with last year. From the perspective of different income levels, the digital economy of high-income countries accounts for 76.9% of the global total. From the perspective of different levels of economic development, the scale of digital economy in developed countries is more than 2.8 times that of developing countries. From the perspective of different economic development levels, the proportion of digital economy GDP in developed countries has reached 51.3%, which is 24.5 percentage points higher than that in developing countries. From the perspective of specific countries, the digital economy of the United States ranks first in the world, reaching 13.1 trillion US dollars. The digital economy of the top five countries

[2] Data Source: China Academy of Information and Communication Technology (CAICT).

[3] Data Source: http://ex.chinadaily.com.cn/exchange/partners/82/rss/channel/cn/columns/j3u3t6/stories/WS5ecb6dbea310eec9c72bb328.html.

[4] Chen Xiaoxi. Digital Intelligence Logistics: Key Technologies and Cases of 5G Supply Chain Reconstruction. China Economic Publishing House, 2020-7.

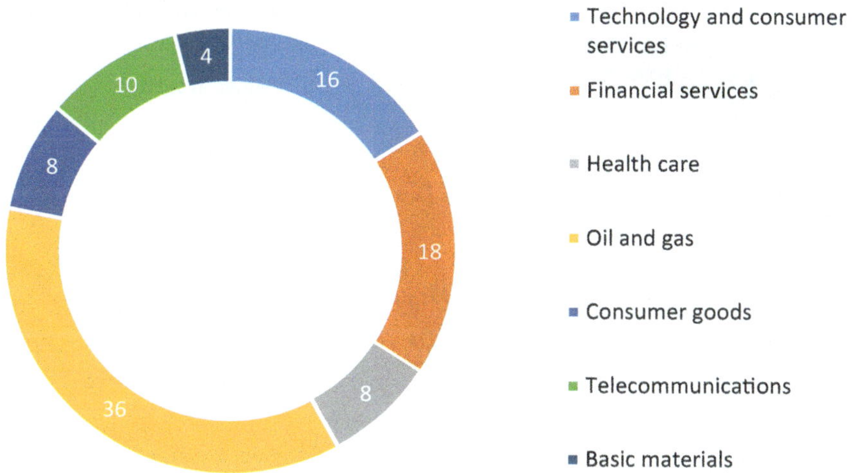

Fig. 1.1 Industry composition of global top 100 listed companies in 2009

accounts for 78.1% of the global total, and the digital economy of Germany, Britain and the United States has accounted for more than 60% of GDP. From the data point of view, the absolute value of growth of digital economy is higher than that of GDP. In 2019, China's digital economy grew rapidly, reaching 35.8 trillion yuan, accounting for 36.2% of China's GDP and contributing 67.7% of the total economic value. The economic added value of digital development of the industry accounted for 80.2% of the economic added value of the entire digital economy.[5]

In terms of specific industries, the two industries, namely, digital platform and industry internet, have outperformed other industries. According to figures from relevant research institutions, China's digital platform will contribute nearly $3 trillion to GDP by 2030.[6] Meanwhile, in terms of industry internet, by 2020, the market size of industry internet is expected to increase to 700 billion yuan.[7] As shown in the comparison of the industry composition of the world's top 100 listed companies in Figs. 1.1 and 1.2, the number of technology and consumer service enterprises has increased significantly. Comparing the 20 companies with the highest market value in the world from the perspective of industry composition, we can see that some large-scale technology companies and digital platforms have become increasingly important in the past decade, and the impact of digital transformation has become the most obvious. In 2009, among the top 20 companies, 7 came from oil and gas industries, accounting for 35% of the total, while only 3 came from technology and consumer services industries (including digital platforms), accounting for only 15% of the total, and the other 3 came from the financial industry. According to the

[5] Digital economy has increased by 35.8 trillion yuan, increasing its contribution rate to GDP growth [J]. China Packaging, 2020, 40(10):10.

[6] Data Source: General Electric.

[7] Data Source: ZhiYan.org.

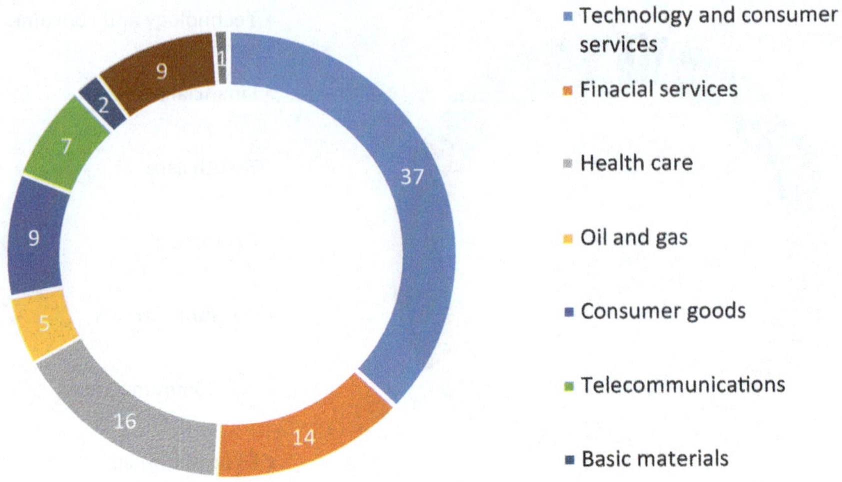

Fig. 1.2 Industry composition of global top 100 listed companies in 2020

industry composition data of the global top 100 listed companies in 2020, among the top 20 enterprises, the number of technology and consumer service enterprises increased to 8, accounting for 40% of the total. And 7 technology and consumer service enterprises ranked in the top ten, while the number of financial enterprises increased to 5. In contrast, only one oil and gas company is still in the top 20. Among the top 10 companies in 2020, Amazon, Alibaba, Facebook and Tencent did not enter the top 100 in 2009.[8]

The United States, as the world's leading digital economy, has a complete industrial chain, which is unmatched by other countries in the short term. The core of the digital economy is chips and operating systems, which are almost monopolized by the United States. From Intel, which occupied an absolute monopoly position in the desktop market in the early days, to Qualcomm, which is unique in the mobile era, and NVIDIA in the field of artificial intelligence. Once the United States stops supplying chips, the global digital economy may be in trouble. In terms of core operating systems, Microsoft occupies more than 90% of the market share in desktop computers, while Google's Android and Apple's IOS systems dominate the mobile terminals. In the field of web search, Google occupies more than 90% market share, while Baidu's market share is almost negligible. In the field of e-commerce, Amazon is the largest e-commerce platform in the world. In terms of cloud business, Amazon is also outstanding. Facebook is the world's largest social network, and Tesla is the world's highest-selling new energy vehicle company. And with the technological progress breaking the limit of growth, the increase of income is more and more obvious, which also makes Matthew effect increasingly prominent. In the past two years, in the top 14 digital economy in the United States, the total market value of listed companies increased from 4045.3 billion US dollars to 5336.3 billion US

[8] Data Source: UNCTAD Digital Economy Report 2018 & PwC Global top 100 companies 2020.

dollars, an increase of about 32%. In the same period, the index rose from 2457 to 2937, an increase of only about 20%.[9]

Due to the impact of the Covid-19, many industries have been hindered in their way, and some are even stagnating. However, industries such as telecommuting, online education, and Internet medical services that are not restricted by location have brought in a new wave opportunity in this epidemic. Data from the WeLink platform shows that more than 15,000 companies have connected to Huawei's telecommuting system on an average day, and online meetings exceed 120,000 times a day, with a daily growth rate of 50%.[10] Similarly, within one month after the outbreak of the epidemic, online medical industry is booming. New users of Ping An Good Doctor, an application in medical industry exceeded 1000%, and the average daily visitors of Ali Health exceeded by more than 500%. The traffic of page clicks of "Ask a Doctor", one app of Baidu hit nearly 200 million times.[11] Many industries in the digital economy are "rising against the trend" in this disaster. Obviously, the digital economy is a key move for countries to promote the rapid recovery of the economy, and has become the potential for world's economic growth.

With the continuous transformation and innovation of digital technology,[12] the production factors are reconstructed and traditional industries escalated towards digital industries. As a result, the platform economy has been grown, so has business environment gradually changed. Traditional market transactions mainly centered on the three factors of production: labor, land, and capital. Nevertheless, with the innovation and application of digital technology, data has become one of the most dynamic production factors in the market. By the end of this year, the world's data scale will exceed the 50ZB mark.[13] The huge amount of data drives the expansion of the traditional business from land, labor, and capital to the range of the digital business environment which aims to build a data transaction platform and ensure data security.

---

[9] Data source: 2019 US Digital Economy Development Report.

[10] Data Source: https://www.ndrc.gov.cn/xwdt/ztzl/jzjj/202009/t20200910_1238047.html.

[11] Data Source: https://www.ndrc.gov.cn/xwdt/ztzl/jzjj/202009/t20200910_1238047.html.

[12] A new generation of digital technology representatives: big data, cloud computing, blockchain, digital twins, artificial intelligence, etc.

[13] Data Source: China Academy of Information and Communication Technology (CAICT). Big Data Development White Paper (2019).

Chapter 2
Concept Scope

Abstract The digital economy needs a good business environment to stimulate its huge dividends, which gives a new concept to the digital business environment. Based on the extensive searching and reading of domestic and foreign valuable researches, we decided to use the bibliometric method to study the digital business environment. Firstly, the scholars' research context was visualized from multiple angles. Secondly, the connotation of the business environment was defined, which had highlighted the new content of the digital business environment. And then we studied different digital business environment evaluation systems. We also analyze the evaluation of the digital business environment from two different aspects: a single-dimensional view of the business environment evaluation index system, and a comprehensive view of the digital business environment evaluation index system. Finally, we reviewed and compared the business environment policy systems of various countries in the world.

2.1 The Concept of the Doing-Digital-Business Environment[1] Is "Ready to Come Out"

Digital economy is expected to bring huge dividends and requires a better business environment to support its growth. As early as 2018, General Secretary Xi pointed out that "the business environment may not call for the best, but for better." After entering 2019, The Fourth Plenary Session of the 19th Central Committee in 2019 also explicitly proposed to "improve the business environment and stimulate the vitality of various market players." In November of the same year, General Secretary Xi pointed out at the opening ceremony of the second China International Import Expo that China should continue to optimize the business environment and he also compared the business environment to the soil for the survival and growth of enterprises. In November this year, General Secretary Xi once again emphasized the necessity to create a better environment with high-quality services at the 3rd China International Import and Export Expo. It can be seen the fact that General

[1] Note: In this paper, doing-business environment and digital business environment has the same concept. The former derives from the meaning of the project of the same name, while the latter is the usual expression.

X. Li et al., *Development Practice of Digital Business Environment in China*, Applied Economics and Policy Studies,
https://doi.org/10.1007/978-981-16-8527-9_2

Secretary Xi Jinping has mentioned the business environment on various important occasions, which fully expresses China's determination to create a fair, just, and non-discriminatory economic environment, and to build a business that gives full play to the market all along, and to uphold justice and the rule of law to be in line with the international standard.

The emergence of the term "Business Environment" can be traced back to 2002. In order to analyze and evaluate the business environment of enterprises with different life cycles from various aspects, the international finance corporation, which owned by the World Bank, thereafter launched the "Doing Business" project. By formulating a set of globally comparable business environment assessment system, the survey provides a certain reference for different countries in the world to create a better business environment. The World Bank defines Doing Business as the total amount of time and cost that an enterprise bears in key areas in the whole production and operation process such as starting a business, financial credit, protecting investors, paying taxes, etc.[2] The World Bank has constructed a set of indicator framework for evaluating the business environment. Since 2003, World Bank has made objective evaluation to each country annually; up to 2020, there have 190 economies and eleven indicators been included in the report. As time goes by, the connotation of business environment is gradually updated, and scholars have a more profound and deep-seated understanding of this term. The specific manifestations could be found in such facets such as the transformation from the investment environment to the business environment, the combination of macro and micro perspectives, and the combination of hard and soft environments and finally they realized that business environment is an organic ecosystem, and under the context of digitalization, business environment is expected to make it more abundant connotation based on the connotation of traditional business environment.

United Nations Conference on Trade and Development (UNCTAD) first gave the definition of "Digital Businesses". In 2017 the report *Developing Digital Industries* was released, and it was proposed that digital businesses should be interpreted from two levels. On the one hand, digital startups should create value by making digitalized innovation so that gain a competitive edge among the whole industry; on the other hand, it refers to the digital platform or digital market, which is inherently monopolistic, obtains greater value and advantage not only by obtaining data from the entire industry but by using intelligent algorithms gain even more. In 2018, the World Bank put forward the "Digital Business Indicators", which believes that a more efficient, convenient and transparent digital business environment should be built to promote healthy competition among countries and further enhance the vitality of the development of the digital economy. The World Economic Forum and Harvard Business Review released the *Doing-Digital-Business Environment Convenience 2019* report, which holds that "Doing Digital Business" refers to the degree of convenience shared by digital platforms in the process of entering, operating, prospering, and exiting the market. In 2019, a report released by Alibaba pointed out that the digital business

[2] World Bank Group. Doing Business 2020 [R]. The World Bank, 2019. https://openknowledge.worldbank.org/bitstream/handle/10986/32436/9781464814402.pdf.

environment should attach great attention on creating a good environment for settled companies, which specifically refers to build a platform of a fair, transparent, and healthy ecology through technology.

The digital business environment should not only be a "digital + business environment" that uses digital technology to transform and upgrade the traditional market environment, but also a "digital business + environment", that is, a new business environment that faces and adapts to needs of the market players to innovate and develop in digital economy (as shown in Fig. 2.1). In the era of digital economy, the government, enterprises, platforms, users and other entities is expected to connect with each other, constantly optimizing production relations to create and share value. To achieve the goal of building an excellent digital business environment and promoting the high-quality development of digital economy, future policies should focus on digital infrastructure, regulation and rule of law construction, tax and government service reform, data security and so on. Although international organizations have different interpretations of the digital business environment, they all attach importance to the difference between digital business and traditional business, maintaining and activating the vitality of the digital economy, and emphasizing the role of the platform as "quasi-public" as the main body of emerging markets in optimizing and upgrading the digital business environment.

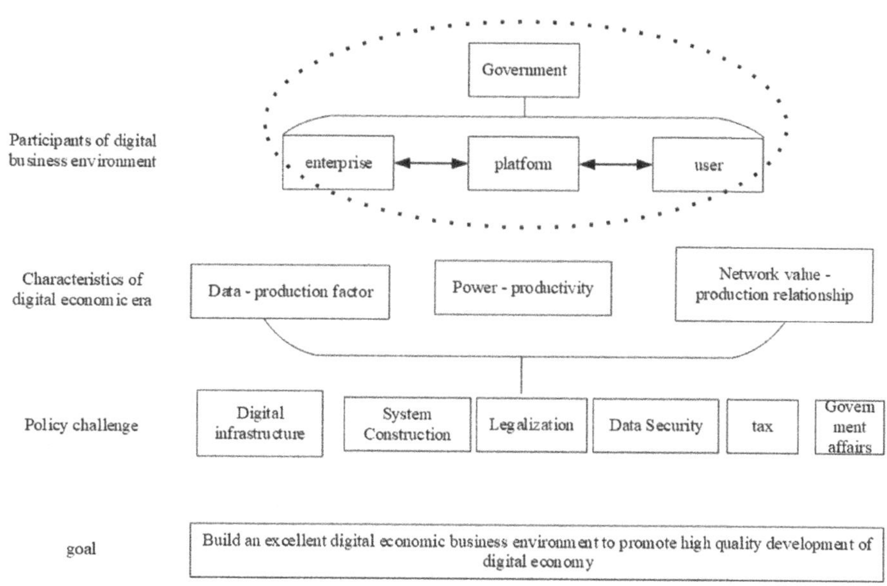

Fig. 2.1 Characteristics and Challenges of digital business environment

2.2 Overview of Researches on Business Environment Based on Bibliometrics

Taking November 5, 2020 as the retrieval point, choose CNKI and WOS database, collect papers related to business environment research, select "old version" and "advanced search" on CNKI, and set the keyword as "business environment". In order to ensure that the collected papers meet the requirements, check the options all included except "All Journals" under the journal subtitle options as the sample. After sorting out, the articles whose organization make it empty and author himself as editorial staff is eliminated, and a total of 429 articles are obtained (including 6 articles related to the theme of digital business environment). In WOS database, the literature type is narrowed to "Article", the literature is searched with "business environment" as the key word, the literature is derived to plain text format, and sift out the repeated literature in CiteSpace, and finally 1105 related articles are obtained. The published quantity of related literatures at home and abroad in recent 23 years is shown in Fig. 2.2, with the growth curve of papers drawn in excel. It can be seen that the number of literature published related with the theme of business environment in China has gradually increased in recent five years, showing an upward trend. The trend regression equation is Y = 610-6E0.7249X, and the determination coefficient R^2 is 0.9; Foreign research on business environment assessment can be traced back to 1997, and the overall published quantity shows a steady upward trend. The regression equation is Y = 1.1943x + 31.112, and the determination coefficient R^2 is 0.5387. It can be seen from comparison at home and abroad that foreign research on business environment is earlier than domestic research, and the research trend is rather stable. Domestic research on business environment started

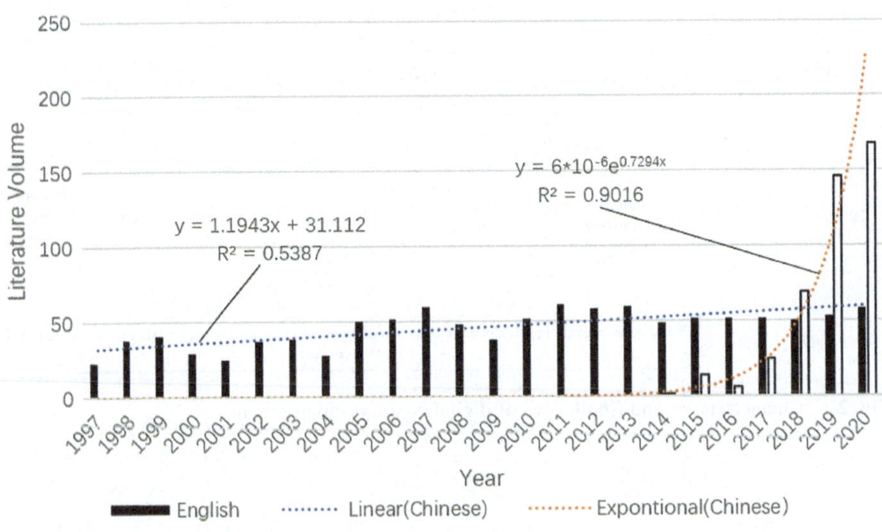

Fig. 2.2 Statistics of published articles from 1997 to 2020

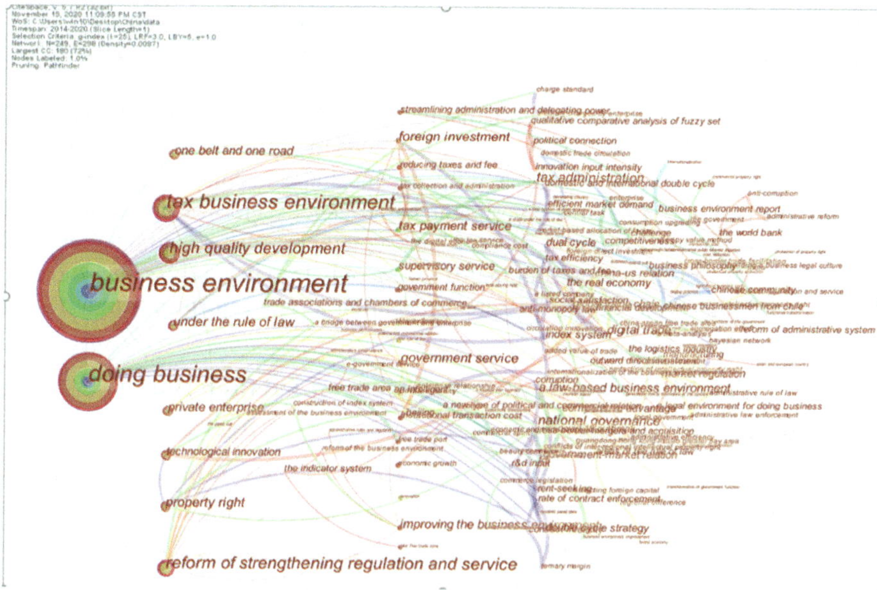

Fig. 2.3 Keyword distribution networks of Chinese research

late. However, the growth momentum is rapid, and the number of published articles shows exponential growth every year, which might be related to the importance attached by various countries to business environment under the background of the globalization of digital economy.

In order to further clarify the research overview in the field of the business environment, CiteSpace is used to process the derived pieces of literatures as well to construct a keywords network. The keyword distribution network of Chinese research is shown in Fig. 2.3.

The centrality of a keyword is reflected by the size of the node. The bigger the node, the stronger the centrality of the keyword. It can be seen that the business environment is the core node, and its centrality is 0.61 which denotes scholars pay great attention to the business environment; three intermediate nodes are "de-regulation reform", high-quality development, tax business environment, with their centrality 0.26, 0.18, and 0.14 respectively, indicating that scholars focus on these aspects of business environment as well. It can be seen from the diagram that there are many edge nodes, which shows that the research topics of business environment are diverse on the one hand, and the research topics are relatively scattered on the other hand. Further studies are found that although the centrality of some edge nodes, such as the World Bank, Doing-Business environment report, and the Doing Business indicator system are relatively low, their degree is very high, indicating that they are hot issues in the field of business environment.

On the basis of the above, the burst point analysis of keywords appearing in the literature database can show the time period when keywords emerge, as shown in Fig. 2.4.

It can be seen from the above figure that there have been four key words in the past 19 years, namely 2003, 2004, 2018 and 2019. Among them, the most key words broke out in 2003: investment site selection, influence mechanism, contract execution rate, contract intensity, quasi-natural experiment, heterogeneity, etc. The key words broke out in 2004 were: new taxes and fees for bankruptcy procedures, and integration of ideas. The key words that broke out in 2018 were only the tax business environment. The key words that broke out in 2019 are distribution service reform and high-quality

Fig. 2.4 Statistics of key words outbreak points in business environment. *Image Source* This image is exported by the author from CiteSpace software

Table 2.1 Q value and S value under different slice length

Slice length	Q value	S value	Slice length	Q value	S value
1	0.7522	0.9499	11	0.8247	0.9307
2	0.7760	0.9429	12	0.8138	0.9298
3	0.7984	0.9516	13	0.8105	0.9104
4	0.7853	0.9440	14	0.8149	0.9321
5	0.8107	0.9461	15	0.793	0.924
6	0.8131	0.9502	16	0.7726	0.9211
7	0.819	0.9395	17	0.7514	0.9107
8	0.7746	0.9229	18	0.819	0.9524
9	0.8207	0.9462	19	0.841	0.9515
10	0.8329	0.9362	-	-	-

development. It can be seen that as the country pays more and more attention to the construction and development of business environment. The policy of distribution service reform aims to promote high-quality economic development.

In order to explore the changing trend of research topics in the field of business environment research, the key words are clustered. On the basis of keyword analysis, different slice length values are selected to get different clustering results. There are two indexes to measure the clustering effect: Q value and S value. Q is the clustering module value, and Q value greater than 0.7 indicates that clustering is credible. The average contour value of clustering is represented by S value, which needs to be greater than 0.7 if the clustering result is to be credible. When setting the keyword clustering step size, we can change Slice length to different time intervals in turn and get Q value and S value (as shown in Table 2.1).

It can be seen from the above table that all S values are above 0.78, which meets the requirements, and Q values are above 0.75. According to Q values, S values and actual clustering effects under different Slice length values, the cluster map with Slice length of 10 is selected, as shown in Fig. 2.5.

It can be seen from Fig. 2.5 that when Slice Length = 10, there are 14 clusters: business environment, private economy, government ruled by law, logistics industry, investment environment, tax reduction and fee reduction, the belt and road initiative, enterprise innovation, World Bank, distribution service reform, foreign direct investment, fair justice, foreign direct investment, and Russia. Further summarizing the clustering results of different Slice lengths, it is found that the results produced by other clusters are subsets of clustering results when Slice length is equal to 10, which also proves that Slice Length = 10 is the best clustering step.

Then, according to the clustering results, the main keywords contained in each cluster are summarized, as shown in Table 2.2.

From the amount of articles published by authors, we can see the amount of articles published by authors and their influence in the subject field. Table 2.3 shows the amount of articles published by the top 10 authors and their cooperation intensity

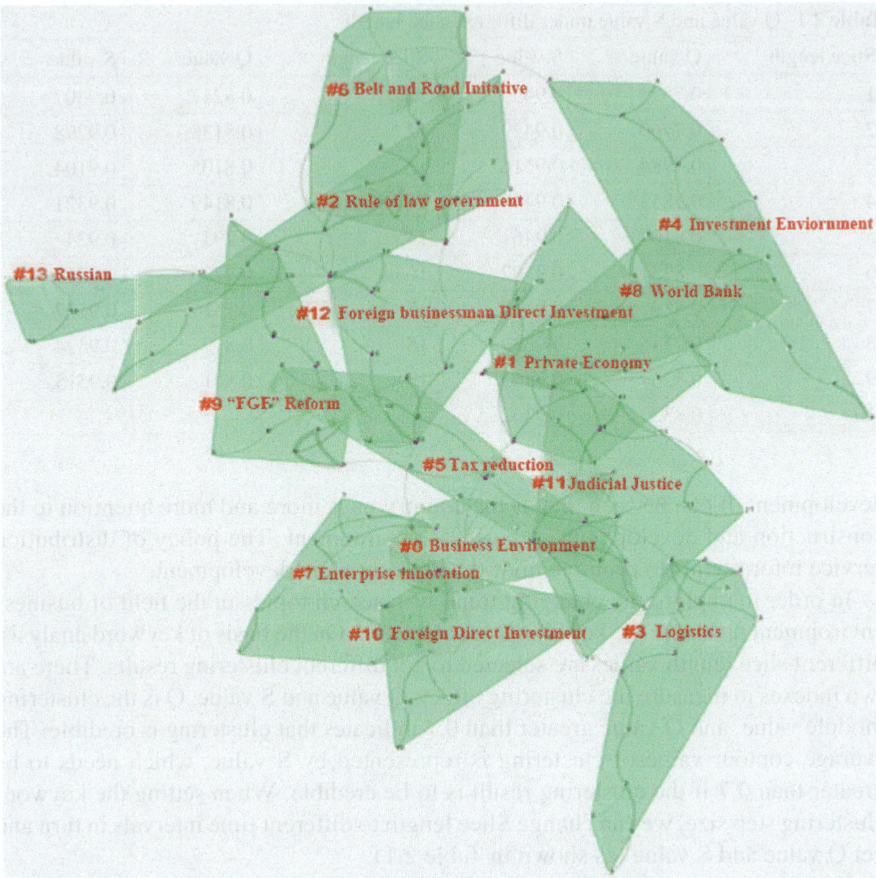

Fig. 2.5 Keyword clustering effect diagram when slice length = 10

with other authors. From Table 2.3, we can see that Zhang Meisha has the largest amount of articles published, Through Table 2.3, we can more intuitively understand the specific amount of articles published by the top 10 authors and their cooperation intensity.

By studying the research institutions where the business environment research authors are located, we can see the institutions with strong scientific research strength and influence in this field. In order to clearly show the amount of articles issued by each institution, we searched the top 10 research institutions in the software background database (see Table 2.4).

It can be seen from the above table that the statistics of published articles are accurate to the secondary units, and the data is consistent with the node size in Fig. 2.3. The School of Economics and Finance of Xi'an Jiaotong University ranks first, with 45 published articles, the School of Economics of Nankai University ranks second with 29 published articles, and the School of Public Administration

Table 2.2 Cluster analysis of literature keywords

Cluster number	Primary coverage	Primary coverage
#1	Private economy	Optimize business environment, tax business environment, international experience, market, export intensity and market supervision
#2	A rule of law government	National governance, administration according to law, business environment ruled by law, and local legislation of commercial system
#3	Logistics industry	Green logistics, logistics upgrading, urban development, smile index, supply side
#4	Investment environment	Trade links, circulation efficiency, fair competition, facilitation, marketization and investment motivation
#5	Cut taxes and administrative fees	Social tax service, tax service, taxpayer satisfaction, digital tax and tax rate level
#6	The Belt and Road Initiative	Countries along the route, global innovation chain, cooperation prospects, free trade, and country differences
#7	Enterprise innovation	Innovation margin, innovation vitality, enterprise R&D investment, government-enterprise relationship, entrepreneur time allocation
#8	World bank	Index framework, subjective perception, third-party perspective, satisfaction, market subject
#9	Reform of distribution suit	Free trade port, individual industrial and commercial households, port opening and trade, mechanism innovation, governance efficiency
#10	FDI	Intensive marginal, uncertainty, investment location, enterprise location factor market
#11	Impartial administration of justice	Administrative law enforcement, efficiency of rule of law, regional rule of law, standardized law enforcement and scientific legislation
#12	Foreign direct investment (FDI)	Economic development, foreign investment policy, urbanization level, city scale and opening to the outside world

(continued)

Table 2.2 (continued)

Cluster number	Primary coverage	Primary coverage
#13	Russia	FdI, Dynamic Panel Data, System GMM, Transaction Cost, Northeast Revitalization

Table 2.3 Top 10 authors and their cooperation intensity

Serial number	Author	Number of posts issued	Cooperation intensity
1	Zhang Meisha	41	1.42
2	Feng Tao	21	1.06
3	Ding Shuang	20	2.0
4	Liu Huizheng	18	1.0
5	Xu Hao	17	1.06
6	Lv Xiangwei	17	1.0
7	Liu Binglian	16	1.0
8	Su Lingran	16	0
9	Luo Min	16	0
10	Dun Shuai	15	2.0

Table 2.4 Statistical table of the number of articles published by research institutions

Serial number	Research institutions	Number of publications
1	Xi'an Jiaotong University School of Economics and Finance	45
2	Nankai University School of Economics	29
3	Renmin University of China School of Public Administration and Policy	23
4	Southwest University College of Economics and Management	18
5	Huaqiao University School of Economics and Finance	18
6	Tongji University School of Economics and Management	18
7	Wuhan University School of Law	18
8	Southwest University Economic Research Center	17
9	Central South University Business School	17
10	Inner Mongolia University School of economics and management	17

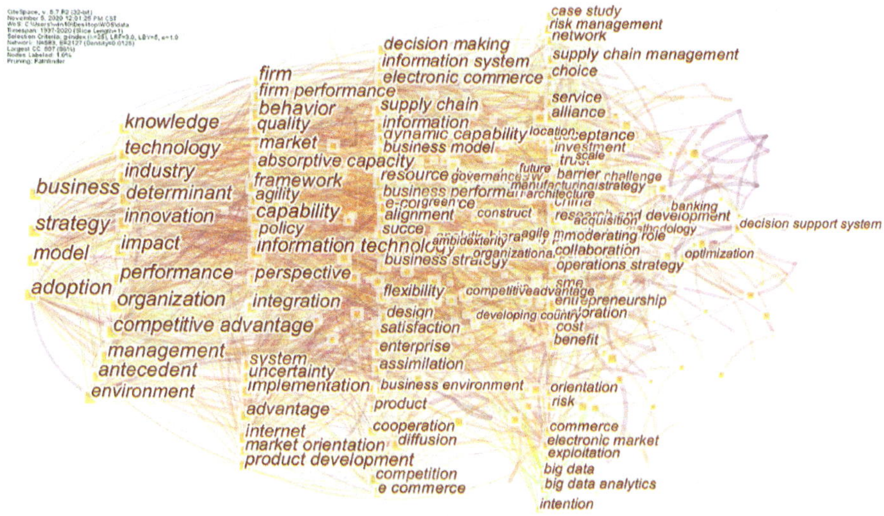

Fig. 2.6 Keywords distribution network of English research

of Renmin University of China ranks third with 23 published articles in the field of business environment. In addition, the number of articles published by research institutions ranked 4–10 is roughly the same.

Considering the fact that the sources of research samples of scholars at home and abroad are rather different and the amount of data is quite distinct, in addition, foreign research started earlier than domestic research. Besides, there are only keywords of English research in the visualization, and the nodes of Chinese research will be marginalized if the data of the two are combined to analyze. Therefore, the relevant research on business environment in English should be also independently analyzed, as shown in Fig. 2.6.

Different from Chinese research, foreign research has four central nodes, namely business, strategy, model, and adoption. Their centrality is 0.12, 0.11, 0.1, and 0.1, respectively, indicating that scholars pay a lot of attention to business and strategy; intermediate nodes are environment, competitive advantage, performance, impact, innovation, organization, etc. with their centrality are 0.09, 0.08, 0.08, 0.07, 0.07, 0.07, respectively, which shows that scholars focus on these aspects of the business environment. It can be seen from the diagram that more nodes between different levels are studied in foreign countries than in Chinese which suggests that the research scope of business environment in foreign countries is more extensive. It is worth noting that the centrality of the business environment is relatively low, but its degree is relatively high. It suggests that there are more researches on the combination of business environment and other topics.

In view of this, this report will conduct literature review of the connotation of business environment and business environment assessment respectively and accordingly predict the trend of the development in the field of business environment.

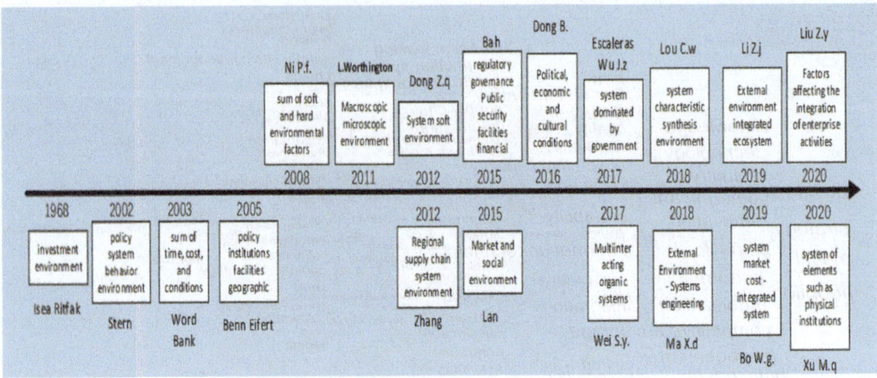

Fig. 2.7 Connotation of business environment

2.3 Connotation of Business Environment

Materialist dialectics believes that everything always has to experience twists and turns as they grow. The interpretation of the term of business environment is a dynamic reflection on the basis of practice. As people's Interpretation of the connotation of business environment varies with the changes over time, at present, the academic community have not yet reached a conclusion on the connotation of business environment. This report screens out the relevant literature of business environment at home and abroad, and combs out the key research on the connotation of business environment through the timeline route, as shown in Fig. 2.7.

As early as 1968, American scholars were the first to use the "cold and hot analysis method" to evaluate the investment environment. From the standpoint of investors and investors, this method comprehensively evaluated the investment country from seven investment environment factors: political stability, market opportunities, economic growth, cultural unity, legal obstacles, substantive obstacles, geographical and cultural differences. The better the investment environment, the stronger the country's investment motivation is, and vice versa.[3]

Since the World Bank released its report in 2003, business environment began to came into public vision. In fact, the term "Doing Business" first appeared in 2002. In order to analyze and evaluate the business environment faced by enterprises in different life cycles from various aspects, the International Finance Corporation of the World Bank launched a project, namely, "Doing Business", which established a globally comparable business environment assessment system, in order to provide reference and basis for different countries to improve the business environment of enterprises. The World Bank defines the Doing Business environment as the sum of the time and cost required by enterprises to comply with policies and regulations in terms of application for establishment, production and operation, trade activities, tax

[3] Deng Hongbing. Investment Environment [M]. Wuhan: China University of Geosciences Press. 2000:1288.

payment, closure and execution of contracts.[4] Stern regards the business environment is concerned with the current and expected policy, system and behavior environment, which is generally related to macroeconomic policies, government administrative system and infrastructure environment, and will affect the investment return and risk of enterprises in turn.[5] Benn Eifert et al. think that business environment is the policy, system, infrastructure, human resources and geographical environment that affect the operational efficiency of an industry and enterprise.[6] Bah & Fang defines the business environment as five aspects: environmental management, corruption management, public security environment, infrastructure rectification degree and financial development.[7] Worthington and Britten claim that the Business environment is the macro environment (politics, economy, law, society, etc.) and micro environment (suppliers, competitors, labor market, financial institutions, etc.), which affect the production and operation of enterprises.[8] Lan claims that the business environment refers to the market and social environment faced by the relevant policies, systems and behavioral norms required by market entities to engage in production and business activities or trade activities.[9] Escaleras & Chiang holds that business environment is the inevitable outcome of government-dominated economy which contains government efficiency, supervision quality and corruption degree, and even the government's market involvement is regarded as part of the business environmental supervision.[10]

The research on "Business Environment" has just sprung up in China, and Guangdong Province, as the pioneer of business environment research, has organized relevant organizations to carry out various research projects.[11] Before the concept of business environment was put forward, there was another synonym: investment environment. This name grew along with the development process of the foreign business environment. It had a high profile at the beginning of China's reform and opening up in the 1980s and 1990s. At that time, it mainly observed the development environment of a region from the perspective of foreign investment, so there was also a saying of investment business environment. Strictly speaking, business environment is a kind of development environment, including soft and hard environment, of which hard environment is material environment, whereas soft environment is an

---

[4] World Bank Group. Doing Business 2020 [R]. The World Bank, 2019. https://openknowledge.worldbank.org/bitstream/handle/10986/32436/9781464814402.pdf.

[5] Stern. *A strategy for development* [M]. Washington: World Bank Publications, 2002.

[6] Benn Eifert, Alan Gelb, Vijaya Ramachand Ran. Business environment and comparative advantage in Africa: evidence from the investment climate data [Z]. ICA World Bank Working Paper, 2005.

[7] Bah E H, Fang L. Impact of the business environment on output and productivity in Africa [J]. Journal of Development Economics, 2015, 114(8), 159–171.

[8] Lan Worthington, Chris Britton. The Business Environment. Economic Management Press, 2011.

[9] Lan Worthington, Chris Britton. The Business Environment 7th Revised Edition [M]. Pearson Education, 2015.

[10] Escale Rasm, Chiang E P. Fiscal decentralization and institutional quality on the business environment [J]. Economics Letters, 2017, 159(8):161–163.

[11] Dong Biao, Li Renyu. Research on the Construction of Legalized International Business Environment in my Country-Based on the Analysis of "Business Environment Report" [J]. Business Economics Research, 2016, (13):141–143.

institutional and cultural environment, so as to constitute the overall development environment of a country or region.[12]

Ni Pengfei divided the business environment into two parts for the first time, including hard environment and soft environment. The hard environment includes market and infrastructure, etc.; while the soft environment includes policy, service, justice, administration and tax system, and so on. Generally speaking, they think that the business environment is the sum of various factors in the production and operation activities of enterprises.[13] However, some scholars believe that the business environment only contains a soft institutional environment, and the government can effectively shape the business environment through a series of policy tools.[14] Zhang, et al. define by extensions of business environment from the perspective of globalization, pointing out that a systematic environment composed of business environment factors which should include regional factors such as labor costs and transportation costs, exchange rates, taxes and tariffs, and supply chain factors such as products and trade.[15] From the perspective of social environment, Dong Biao and Li Renyu claim that business environment refers to various situations and conditions, in which market entities engage in commercial organizations or business operations, including political factors, economic factors and cultural factors that affect the behavior of market entities. It is the basis for a country or region to effectively carry out culture exchanges, cooperation and participate in competition, displaying its economic soft power.[16] Wu Jingzhou pointed out that the business environment is essentially the government's regulatory environment, and the offside, absence and dislocation of the government will affect the business environment in turn.[17] Wei Shuyan and Sun Feng consider that the investment and business environment is an organic dynamic system, in which contains political system, economy and market, social culture, policies and regulations and other factors that interact and influence with each other.[18]

---

[12] Lou Chengwu, Zhang Guoyong. Research on the Construction of Business Environment Assessment Framework Based on the Subjective Perception of the Market Subject: A Review of Business Environment Assessment Model of the World Bank [J]. Contemporary Economic Management, 2018, 40(06):60–68.

[13] Ni Pengfei. What do Chinese cities attract investors [J]. Management Consulting, 2008 (1): 102–105.

[14] Dong Zhiqiang, Wei Xiahai, Tang Canqing. Institutional Soft Environment and Economic Development-An Empirical Study Based on the Business Environment of 30 Big Cities [J]. Management World, 2012 (4): 9–20.

[15] Zhang A, Huang G Q, Liu X, Impacts of Business Environment Changes on Global Manufacturing in The Chinese Greater Pearl River Delta: A Supply Chain Perspective [J], Applied Economics, 2012, 44, pp. 4505–4514.

[16] Dong Biao, Li Renyu. Research on the Construction of Legalized International Business Environment in my Country Based on the Analysis of "Business Environment Report" [J]. Business Economics Research, 2016, (13):141–143.

[17] Wu Jingzhou. The Revitalization of Northeast China should Start with an Optimized Business Environment [J]. Economic Review, 2017, (1):31–35.

[18] Wei Shuyan, Sun Feng. Evaluation and optimization of investment and business environment in Northeast China [J]. Changbai Journal, 2017, (6): 84–92.

Lou Chengwu believes that the business environment is the development environment faced by market entities in a region, which includes government environment, market environment, legal environment, infrastructure environment, element environment, etc.[19] It is the external manifestation of various formal systems provided by the government and various existing informal systems. Ma Xiangdong and Wang Yuesheng hold that business environment generally refers to the sum of various external environments such as political environment, economic environment, legal environment and international environment in which enterprises are in the process of starting, operating and canceling, and moreover, it is a systematic project involving with many fields in the process of economic and social reform and opening to the outside world.[20] Li Zhijun, et al. believe that the business environment is a comprehensive ecosystem of the external environment faced by enterprises when they engage in entrepreneurship, innovation, financing, investment and other activities, including the resource conditions and environmental conditions faced by enterprises in the whole life cycle, such as capital, talents, technology, policies, etc., specifically including government service efficiency, public services, financial and credit services, human resources, innovation environment and market environment.[21] Some scholars believe that there are many unavoidable links in the process of enterprise establishment and operation: institution, market, business cost, infrastructure, ecology, etc.[22] Similarly, Liu Zhiyong regards the business environment as a systematic project, but it embodies many factors to form a more complicated whole which includes the factors such as system, rule of law and credit, whereas it is different from simple institutional environment, legal environment and credit environment[23] Xu Mingqiang, et al. hold that the business environment is an organic system containing many elements such as material, system, society and relationship network, from which each could constitute various internal and external systems.[24]

It can be seen that scholars have different definitions of business environment, and each scholar defines the connotation of business environment based on his own

---

[19] Lou Chengwu, Zhang Guoyong. Research on the Construction of Business Environment Assessment Framework Based on the Subjective Perception of the Market Subject: A Review of Business Environment Assessment Model of the World Bank [J]. Contemporary Economic Management, 2018, 40(06):60–68.

[20] Ma Xiangdong, Wang Yuesheng. New Policy of Attracting Foreign Investment in the New Era: From Providing Preferential Policies to Improving Business Environment [J]. Journal of the Party School of the Central Committee of the C.P.C, 2018(22).

[21] Li Zhijun, Zhang Shiguo, Li Yifei, Shan Shan. *The Environmental Evaluation of Doing Business in Chinese Cities* and Related Suggestions [J]. Jiangsu Social Sciences, 2019, (2):30–42, 257.

[22] Bo Wenguang, Zhou Yanyu, Lu Dingkun. Entrepreneurship, Business Environment and Corporate Total Factor Productivity-Based on the Analysis of Microdata of Listed Companies in China [J]. Journal of Business Economics, 2019(8):85–97.

[23] Liu Zhiyong, Wei Lili. A Review of Business Environment Construction in China: Development Track, Main Achievements and Future Direction [J]. Contemporary Economic Management, 2020(2):22–27.

[24] Xu Mingqiang, Dong Dahai. Research on the Composition Dimensions and Influencing Factors of the Business Environment on China Free Trade Zone [J]. Journal of Management Case Studies, 2020, 13(4):460–475.

research perspective. Although there is no uniform definition of business environment at present, it has become a consensus that business environment is an important factor that affects the development of enterprises. With the deepening of scholars' understanding of business environment and its connotation become more extensive, the term business environment is embodied in the following aspects: transformation from investment environment to business environment, the integration of macro and micro perspectives, the combination of hard environment and soft environment, and finally come to realize that business environment is an organic ecosystem.

Under the context of digital economy, with digital trade driving industrial transformation, intelligent manufacturing being concerned as the target of industrial manufacturing, that is, another widening path of traditional trade in the era of digital economy, the business environment has a brand-new connotation: digital business environment. Different from the meaning of the traditional business environment, the World Economic Forum and Harvard Business Review released the report "*Doing-Digital-Business environment Convenience 2019*", which holds that "Doing Digital Business" refers to the convenience enjoyed by digital platforms in the process of entering, operating, prospering and exiting the market.[25] As an Internet platform enterprise, Alibaba Group believes that the focus of "Doing Digital Business Environment" is to provide a good environment for settled enterprises and promote to build a platform with a fair, transparent and healthy ecosystem by means of technology.[26] Digital business environment should not simply be a "digital + business environment" to transform and upgrade the traditional market environment by taking advantage of digital technology, but a "digital business + environment", that is, a new business environment facing and adapting to the requirements of the main entities for the sake of innovation and development in the digital economy market. As far as the digital business environment concerned, the main evaluation dimensions are as follows: digital infrastructure, security system, digital market order, digital government services, digital innovation and personnel training, and digital market scale.

2.4 Researches on Business Environment Assessment

In 2001, the World Bank took the lead in setting up a business environment assessment team to assess the business environment of enterprises among the world economies. In 2003, the World Bank released the first report *Doing Business*. Up to now, its indicators have increased to 11 items, and 49 secondary indicators are included under the first-level ones. Scholars at home and abroad basically conduct research follow the lead of the World Bank's *Doing Business* report, from which can be summarized into

25 Global Competitiveness Report 2019: How to end a lost decade of productivity growth. http://www3.weforum.org/docs/WEF_TheGlobalCompetitivenessReport2019.pdf.

26 Alibaba Doing Digital Business Environment in 2019 https://max.book118.com/html/2019/0603/6042222141002034.shtm

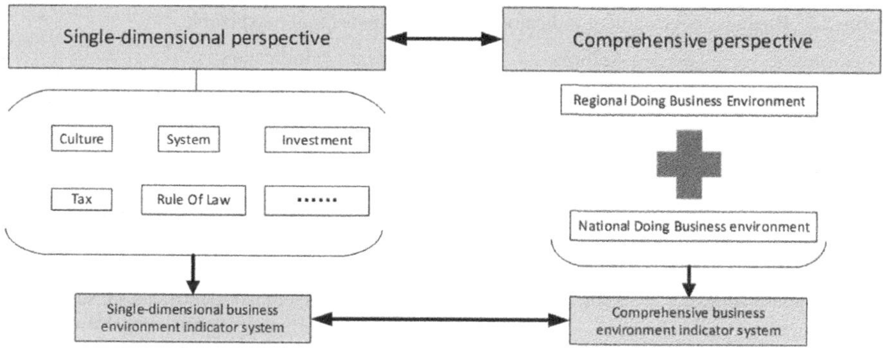

Fig. 2.8 Perspective of business environment indicator system

two major perspectives: one-dimensional perspective and comprehensive perspective. The development process of one-dimensional perspective and comprehensive perspective of research is shown in Fig. 2.8.

One-dimensional perspective refers to the evaluation of a certain aspect of the business environment, such as taxation, rule of law, culture and so on. In terms of taxation, Wang Shaole established an indicator system from four dimensions: rule of law indicator, efficiency indicator, cost indicator and satisfaction indicator, and he took Guangdong Province as an example to make an empirical study based on that system.[27] Li Cheng et al. give an analysis on the taxation indicator of WB' indicator system, and consider that the World Bank did not pay attention to factors such as tax incentives, time costs, national diversities in circumstances and entrepreneurs' own qualities.[28] From the perspective of government affairs, Peng Xianggang et al. constructed four dimensions of evaluation indicators, namely, demand identification, service function, service capability and service supply, which could be applied to the universal evaluation framework.[29] Zheng Fanghui et al. put forward four dimensions, namely, business legal system, business law enforcement, business justice and business law-abiding.[30] As for the evaluation indicator system, Xie Hongxing put forward evaluation indicators of business environment from the angle of rule of law, which contains five aspects, namely, the formulation of laws and regulations, administration in accordance with the law, justice, credit and society.[31]

[27] Wang Shaole, Liu Zhonghu. Study on the Measurement of Chinese Tax Business Environment [J]. Journal of Guangdong University of Finance & Economics, 2014, 29(3):33–39.

[28] Li Cheng, Shi Wenpo. A Study of the World Bank's "Paying Taxes "Indicator System [J]. Journal of Xiamen University (Art & Social Sciences), 2020, (5):118–130.

[29] Peng Xianggang, ma ran. Optimization of Government Business Environment and Construction of Evaluation Index System [J]. Academic Research, 2018, (11):55–61.

[30] Zheng Fanghui, Wang Zheng, Wei Hongzheng. The Rule-of-Law Index of Business Environment: An Evaluation System and A Case Study in Guangdong [J]. Social Science in Guangdong, 2019(5).

[31] Xie Hongxing. China's Mode and Mystem of Business Legal Environment Evaluation-Based on the Perspective of Rule of Law [J] Hubei Social Sciences, 2019(3).

Table 2.5 Business environment indicator from one-dimensional perspective

Perspectives	Authors	Year	Indicators
Tax business environment	Wang Shaole et al.	2014	Rule of law index, efficiency index, cost index and satisfaction index
	Li Cheng et al.	2020	Tax preference, time undertaking, national conditions difference, intermediary market, entrepreneur's own quality
Government business environment	Peng Xianggang et al.	2018	Demand identification, service function, service capability and service supply
Business environment ruled by law	Zheng Fanghui et al.	2019	Legal environment, law enforcement environment, judicial environment and law-abiding environment
	Xie Hongxing	2019	Environment for formulating laws and regulations, administration according to law, justice, credit and society
Business environment of insurance industry	Sun Wujun et al.	2020	Policy, rule of law, honesty, investment/operation, talent tax, cognition, public opinion
Logistics business environment	Huang Yuyi et al.	2019	Logistics demand, development facilities, development environment, operation convenience, operation cost and government support

Some scholars set up Doing business indicators from the whole industry sector perspective. Sun Wujun et al. set up an evaluation system of China's insurance business environment from eight aspects: policy, rule of law, honesty, investment, talents, taxes and fees, public opinion and cognition, and took Jiangsu Province as a sample for empirical analysis.[32] Huang Yuyi et al. set up an evaluation indicator system of urban logistics business environment from six aspects: urban logistics demand, logistics development facilities, logistics development environment, business convenience, business cost and government support.[33] Table 2.5 summarizes the specific contents of the evaluation indicators system.

Comprehensive perspective refers to constructing a multi-dimensional indicators system in order to evaluate the business environment from a wide scope of business environment; meanwhile, by means of reading relevant literature of scholars, it can

[32] Nanjing University Research Group. The Construction of Business Environment Evaluation System of Insurance Industry in China-Based on an Applied Analysis of Jiangsu Province [J]. Insurance Studies, 2020, (5):34–49.

[33] Huang Yuyi, Hu Han. Theoretical Study on Business Environment Evaluation of Urban Logistics [J]. Business Economics Research, 2019, (13):91–93.

be drawn that Doing Business indicators are set from two levels, namely regional perspective, national perspective.

From the regional level, Peng Diyun conducted the business environment assessment in the Yangtze River Economic Belt, and the indicators are included economy, market, infrastructure and policy, and he found that the indicators score of business environment gradually ascended from west to east.[34] Gu Xueqin selected four first-class indicators, namely, government service, industrial transformation, regional function and talent environment in the Yangtze River Delta region, and the research determined the weight of the indicators by entropy weight method by scoring them comprehensively. The conclusion was drawn that Shanghai had the best business environment.[35] Zhang Sanbao made a quantitative analysis of the business environment in China's provinces from four dimensions: market, government affairs, legal policy and humanities. The results indicate that the business environment in China's provinces has hierarchical characteristics.[36] Yang Tao et al. compared the business environment of Jiangsu, Shandong, Guangdong and Anhui provinces from three aspects of market, policy and law, and found that there was no significant difference among the four provinces in the first-level indicators.[37] Ding Ding et al. constructed an evaluation indicator system of urban business environment from six aspects: government environment, public environment, financial environment, human resources, innovation environment and market environment, and selected relevant cities for empirical research. The results indicate that there are great differences in the business environment of different cities.[38] Radukic & Stankovic analyzed the business environment of 17 cities in Serbia, and put forward some suggestions to promote foreign investment accordingly, such as developing regional economy, simplifying the examination and approval procedures for starting a business, etc.[39] Tang Leilei designed questionnaires to obtain data from five aspects: market environment, policy and government environment, social service environment, financing

---

[34] Peng Diyun, Chen Bo, Liu Zhijia. Construction and Application of Regional Business Environment Evaluation Index System-Taking Yangtze River Economic Belt as an Example [J]. Finance and Economics, 2019, (5):49–55.

[35] Gu Xueqin, Li Yudong, Yu Hongxin. Policy measures and effect evaluation of business environment in the Yangtze River Delta [J]. China Business and Market, 2020, 34(6):86–95.

[36] Zhang Sanbao, Kang Bicheng, Zhang Zhixue. Evaluation of Doing Business in Chinese Provinces: Indicator System and Quantitative Analysis [J]. Business Management Journal, 2020, 42(4):5–19.

[37] Yang Tao. Study on the Construction of Business Environment Evaluation Index System-Based on the Comparative Analysis of Shandong, Jiangsu, Zhejiang and Guangdong Provinces [J]. Business Economics Research, 2015, (13):28–31.

[38] Ding Ding, Gao Qiang, Li Xianxiang. The course and evaluation of urban business environment construction in China-taking 36 provincial capitals, municipalities directly under the central government and cities with separate plans as examples [J]. Macroeconomic Management, 2020, (1):55–66.

[39] Radukic S, Stankovic J. Evaluation of Local Business Environment in The Republic of Serbia [J]. Procedia Economics & Finance, 2015, (19):353–363.

environment and legal environment, and analyzed the business environment of small and medium-sized enterprises in Dalian.[40]

At the national level, Pavel Körner et al. made a quantitative study to compare the business environment of Czech Republic and Hungary, whose specific dimensions contain corruption perception, comprehensive governance, capture, opacity and corporate governance risk.[41] Zhang Dahai et al. built an evaluation indicator system of business environment based on four aspects: government and legal environment, economic environment, social and cultural environment and technological environment, and they found that the business environment in China has been improved with each passing year.[42] Lou Wenqian and the kind used the business database and the World Bank business indicators to evaluate the business environment of 62 countries along the Belt and Road Initiative, and then classified the business environment of countries along the route.[43] On the basis of analyzing the evaluation indicator system of business environment in Russia, India, Singapore and Hong Kong, Li Qingchi proposed that the indicator system should be constructed to meet the needs of China's reform practice and market entities should participate in the process of economic reform.[44] Hamlová et al., based on the business environment assessment data of the World Bank in 2013, constructed an evaluation indicator system from two aspects: the intensity degree of legal regulation and the complexity and cost of the regulation process. In addition, they analyzed the reasons for the low ranking of the business environment in the Czech Republic.[45] Table 2.6 lists the specific indicators of business environment at different levels.

To sum up, business indicators varies in a single-dimensional perspective and a comprehensive perspective for the sake of research perspective. While the two research perspectives focus put particular emphasis, the two have positive relation and learn from each other. The assessment indicator system mostly contains the hard environment and soft environment based on the connotation of business environment. Although there are many business environment assessment indicators that have already existed now and the indicator system has been continuously improved, it barely has a universal assessment system considering the distinctive national conditions of various countries. At the same time, there are also indicators under different dimensions that are still repeated and redundant. Hence, based on this scenario the

---

[40] Dong Leilei. Analysis of Dalian City Small and Medium-sized Enterprise Business Environment [D]. Dongbei University of Finance & Economics, 2012.

[41] Pavel Körner, Z.Kudrna, O.Vychodil. Measuring Business Environment Quality in Central Europe [J]. Finance a Uver, 2002, (12):674–697.

[42] Zhang Dahai, Zhu Zhichuan. Evaluation of China's business environment based on factor analysis and entropy method [J]. Accounting Monthly, 2019, (18):124–130.

[43] Lou Wenqian, Pei Lingling. Comprehensive Evaluation of National Business Environment along "the Belt and Road Initiative" [J]. Statistics and Decision, 2020, 36(14):152–156.

[44] Li Qing-chi. Study on the Construction and Application of Business Environment Evaluation Index [J]. Administrative Management Reform, 2018 (9): 76–81.

[45] Hamlov á E, Provazn í kov á K. Assessment of the business environment competitiveness in the Czech Republic and EU [J]. Procedia—Social and Behavioral Sciences, 2014, 109:1225–1229.

Table 2.6 Business environment evaluation indicators at different levels

Perspectives	Authors	Year	Indicators
Evaluation at regional level	Peng Diyun et al.	2019	Economic environment, market environment, infrastructure and supporting environment
	Gu Xueqin et al.	2020	Government services, industrial transformation, regional functions, and talent environment
	Zhang Sanbao et al.	2020	Market environment, government affairs environment, legal policy environment and humanistic environment
	Yang Tao	2015	Market development environment, policy and government affairs environment, and scientific and technological innovation environment
	Ding Ding et al.	2020	Government affairs, public environment, financial services, human resources, innovation environment and market environment
	Radukic S et al.	2015	Economic development strategy, licensing system, financial stability, and the development of public–private partnership
	Tang Leilei	2012	Market environment, policy and government environment, socialized service environment, financing environment and legal environment
Evaluation at national level	Pavel Körner et al.	2002	Corruption perception index, comprehensive governance index, capture index, opacity index and corporate governance risk index

(continued)

Table 2.6 (continued)

Perspectives	Authors	Year	Indicators
	Zhang Dahai et al.	2019	Government and legal environment, economic environment, social and cultural environment and technological environment
	Lou Wenqian and others	2020	World Bank Indicator System
	Li Qingchi	2018	Research on evaluation indicators, actual needs of enterprises, promotion of reform and innovation, follow-up evaluation, and inclusion in performance appraisal
	Hamlov et al.	2014	The intensity of legal regulation and the complexity of the regulation process

future research should give a more detailed analysis based on the digital economy's characteristic.

2.5 Countries Continuously Perfect Policy System and Optimize the Doing-Digital-Business Environment

The popularization of information technology has witnessed the change of the Doing-Business environment. Countries gradually realized the importance of digital business environment, and constantly issued multi-dimensional and multi-system documents to encourage the business environment, so that country's digital business convenience indicator can be improved (take examples of the countries or economies in the forefront of digital business environment convenience assessed by the World Bank, such as New Zealand, Singapore, the European Union, etc.) (Table 2.7).

Through the analysis of the above table, it can be seen that:

(i) New Zealand has the best business environment in the world. New Zealand's economy is highly market-oriented and legalized, with transparent and efficient government management, political stability and social security, and developed communication, highway, railway, shipping and energy networks. Therefore, in the ranking of business environment published by the World Bank, it ranks first all the year round, especially in starting a business, protecting investors and obtaining credit.

Table 2.7 Top countries in the global business environment from 2010 to 2019

Ranking	2019	2018	2017	2016	2015	2014	2013	2012	2011	2010
1	New Zealand	New Zealand	New Zealand	Singapore	Singapore	Singapore	Singapore	Singapore	Singapore	Singapore
2	New Zealand	New Zealand	New Zealand	New Zealand	New Zealand	Hong Kong	Hong Kong	Hong Kong	Hong Kong	New Zealand
3	Denmark	Denmark	Denmark	Denmark	Hong Kong	New Zealand	New Zealand	New Zealand	New Zealand	Hong Kong
4	Hong Kong	South Korea	Hong Kong	South Korea	Denmark	U.S.A	U.S.A	U.S.A	Britain	U.S.A
5	South Korea	Hong Kong	South Korea	Hong Kong	South Korea	Denmark	Denmark	Denmark	U.S.A	Britain
6	Georgia	U.S.A	Norway	Britain	Norway	Malaysia	Norway	Norway	Denmark	Denmark
7	Norway	Britain	Britain	U.S.A	U.S.A	South Korea	Britain	Britain	Canada	Ireland
8	U.S.A	Norway	U.S.A	Sweden	Britain	Georgia	South Korea	South Korea	Norway	Canada
9	Britain	Georgia	Sweden	Norway	Finland	Norway	Georgia	Iceland	Ireland	Australia
10	Macedonia	Sweden	Macedonia	Finland	Australia	Britain	Australia	Ireland	Australia	Norway

Data source world bank

(ii) The developed countries in Europe and America, represented by Britain and the United States, have a relatively high and stable overall business environment. European and American countries, such as Britain and the United States, belong to the series of developed countries in OCED, and have entered the post-industrialization period. Their economic aggregates have always been in the forefront of the world, and they have formed a set of relatively perfect systems and mature rules in the construction of business environment, which has great advantages compared with emerging market economies such as China.

UFB (Ultra-Fast Broadband), the national broadband project launched by New Zealand in 2009, has rapidly improved domestic broadband coverage and provided a good and stable facility foundation for the development of digital economy.[46] In addition, the free trade policy pursued by the New Zealand government has also stimulated the vitality of the domestic digital economy market. At present, the average import tariff of New Zealand with an overall low level at 4.1%, the foreign trade regulation is relatively loosened, the import license is cancelled, and electronic customs clearance is greatly encouraged. Furthermore, it enthusiastically supports exports by means of establishing the New Zealand Trade and Enterprise (NZTE) and putting various bonuses, funds and credit guarantees in order to help enterprises. At the same time, in terms of investment policy, the New Zealand government actively encouraged to absorb much outside investment. Except for the areas in nuclear technology, genetically modified technology and other publicly prohibited zone, no more other areas were prohibited to admitting into the country. It treats domestic and foreign investors without discrimination with sharing the same regulation when it concerns with tax policies and loans. It is worth mentioning that the New Zealand government has high administrative efficiency. In 2019, New Zealand Prime Minister Adeen announced that he would devote himself to building a Business Connect, a digital service platform, making it easier for small enterprises to obtain services from multiple government agencies, and giving enterprises more time to focus on their own priorities.[47]

In order to help small businesses develop and promote the overall business environment of the society, the New Zealand government has made great efforts to provide specific assistance to small business owners at various levels. First of all, entrepreneurs can find detailed statistical data in Statistics New Zealand and the local government, and use these statistical data to help them conduct market research and understand the overall situation of their industry, so as to grasp business opportunities. If the public data on the Internet is not enough, entrepreneurs can also contact the Statistics Bureau directly, and let the Statistics Department provide corresponding statistical data specifically for their needs. Most of these services are free of charge, and only in rare cases do they need to pay a certain fee, but they are all affordable.

Secondly, there are a number of business-related ministerial positions in the Cabinet of the New Zealand Government to take charge of different service work. For example, ministers of small enterprises, economic development, employment,

---

[46] Source: http://news.163.com/16/0420/09/BL38RVC700014AED.html.

[47] Source: http://nz.mofcom.gov.cn/article/jmxw/201907/20190702882024.shtml.

economic development in remote areas, scientific research and innovation, state-owned enterprises, trade and export growth, etc., provide help for enterprise development at different levels. The contact information of ministers is open, and business owners can directly talk with ministers and report the situation to them. In addition, many government departments and social welfare organizations regularly hold symposiums and experience sharing meetings for enterprises, which are free of charge and can provide enterprises with one-stop policy consulting services in human resources, taxation, social insurance, financial support, legal compliance and other aspects.

Thirdly, the government provides practical help for enterprises. New Zealand is a country with foreign trade and exports as its main sources of GDP, so its government has given great support to increasing exports. The New Zealand Trade Development Board also has a team dedicated to promoting exports. Their work is very specific: to help enterprises connect customers, provide resources for enterprises, and help enterprises find markets. The only purpose is to enable enterprises to earn foreign exchange by export faster and better. This year, the New Zealand Trade Development Board also personally came forward to organize more than 20 food enterprises and opened the New Zealand National Flagship Store on Tmall to promote New Zealand food. It is rare in the world for the New Zealand government to give such support to export enterprises.

Singapore, which ranks second in the world for the sake of business environment, in early year started to pay attention to the significant area in the national economy, that is, information industry, and it focus on the development of software and links in the information and communication industry. At the same time, the Singapore government has established a set of sound financial and modern service systems and correspondingly matched legal systems which provided efficient services for business activities of enterprises. The Singapore government has also created a pro-business environment with few taxes, simple tax laws and low tax rates. With low rate of income tax at 17%, Singapore is one of the countries with the lowest tax rates in the world. Owning to its dominant position as Asian financial center, more than 500 local and foreign related financial institutions have contributed a lot of financial products and services to Singapore, which has brought convenience to enterprises' financing behavior. In addition, Singapore also attaches great importance to the protection of intellectual property rights, and has joined various world cooperation organizations and signed treaties to protect the interests of enterprises, such as the international treaties on trade-related intellectual property rights, thus creating a good foundation for its innovative milieu.

For many years, Singapore has been ranked among the best in the business environment, and its excellent experience in shaping the world-class business environment has important reference significance for other countries to upgrade their own business environment. To sum up, Singapore's good business environment benefits from its advantages in government affairs, business and legal environment.

First of all, Singapore is committed to creating a clean and efficient government environment and a one-stop government service system. On the one hand, Singapore has a world-leading e-government system, and citizens can easily visit government websites and access thousands of online service functions. "Unified Service" enables people to report various community affairs through mobile applications. Unified information allows the public to save personal information and certification materials, and call them when applying for various online services. Pay attention to the equalization of digital government services and set up a "citizen contact center". Promote the construction of a single window of national trade. TradeNet system connects 35 government departments related to international trade in Singapore, including customs bureau and port authority. In addition, the Singapore government has invested in or participated in the construction of e-government platforms such as PortNet, MariNet and Cargo Community Network, which further enriched the content and coverage of a single window. On the other hand, Singapore is committed to the construction of a clean system, with a clean political culture, strict anti-corruption laws and strong anti-corruption institutions, and is one of the cleanest economies in the world.

Secondly, Singapore has convenient and open business conditions, and its market openness ranks first in the country. A considerable number of industries are completely open to foreign investment, and foreign investment is given national treatment without limiting the proportion of foreign equity. The procedures for registering companies are also very simple, and generally only need to register with the State Administration of Accounting and Enterprise. As mentioned above, Singapore is one of the countries with low tax burden in the world, and all enterprises can enjoy tax-free treatment of the first 300,000 Singapore dollars taxable income, with consumption tax rate of 7% and personal income tax rate between 0 and 22%. In terms of convenience, Singapore's production and operation facilities are complete, with well-equipped commercial parks and industrial parks for enterprises to settle down. Investors can apply for permanent residency or business entry permits. Singapore has no foreign exchange control, and capital is highly free to enter and exit. The basic policy for investment is to "manage in and leave out". For capital outflow, it is not necessary to report to the government or obtain permission in advance. In terms of investment promotion system, Singapore has a single competent Unit-Economic Development Bureau (EDB), which is responsible for formulating and implementing preferential policies to attract foreign investment and providing efficient administrative services. With one-stop full-process service, it not only provides "full-process" services such as prior consultation-policy docking-project landing-follow-up supporting, but also participates in coordinating specific links of production and operation such as science and technology, taxation, employment and labor security. An investment and financing project corresponds to an EDB specialist, and one-to-one management is carried out to ensure that investors are provided with high-quality, efficient and systematic consultation.

Finally, Singapore has a fair and strict legal system, which inherits the English legal system and has complete economic laws and regulations, and a large number of international rules are adopted in commercial laws and regulations. The Free Trade Zone Law is the core law of Singapore's free trade zone operation, which comprehensively stipulates the institutional arrangements of the free trade zone, including positioning, functions, management system, preferential policies, supervision system and many other aspects. The Singapore government set up a regulatory review team as early as 2002, and then upgraded to a "Smart Regulatory Commission" in 2005, requiring all regulations implemented by public departments to be reviewed every 3–5 years to ensure that the regulations keep pace with the changes in the market environment and continuously improve the quality of business supervision.

Since the beginning of the twentieth century, European countries have started to build network infrastructure and made great efforts to promote ICT connectivity and service in European countries. The European Parliament passed the *European Service Industry Directive* in 2006, requiring all member countries to establish digital portals.[48] In 2010, the European Union officially issued the *European Digital Agenda*, put forward the optimization move to tackle with the current obstacles in the process of improving information technology in Europe,[49] and set a goal with broadband network coverage in fast (30 Mbps or higher) speed and ultra-high-speed (100 Mbps or higher) by the year of 2020. As of February 2019, the EU has issued 162 urging decisions on digital infrastructure construction.[50]

In addition to policies to encourage the construction and investment of network infrastructure, European countries have also put forward a series of policies and measures related to the value-added chain in digital economy. The European Commission submitted a digital single market strategy in 2005, which triggered many specific initiatives in the digital field: *Digital European Industry* (DEI) Initiative (2016) put forward a series of policies to promote the digital industry. The European Gigabit Broadband Strategic Plan (2016) proposed a risk financing mechanism to promote 5G innovation and industry participation and public capital investment. *The General Data Protection Regulations* (GDPR) formulated in 2018 supplemented the laws and regulations related to privacy and data security, and further standardized the development of data industry and digital economy.[51] In addition, the European Union launched the *Education and Training 2010 Plan* (ET2010) in the field of education and training, which shed lights on the EU's digital core literacy capacity and cultivating talents' digital literacy capacity.

Each country literally plays the similar game in optimizing digital business environment. Most of them start from the construction of network infrastructure, continuously improve the network coverage, network bandwidth and network speed in their own countries, and then rely on the established network infrastructure to implement and promote various Internet applications (government service platform, electronic customs clearance, etc.). At the same time, under the context of digital economy they

---

[48] Evert-Jan Mulder, Dhoya Snijders, Playing the telephone game in a multilevel polity: On the implementation of e-government services for business in the EU, Government Information Quarterly, 2020, 101526, ISSN 0740-624X.

[49] Source: http://www.most.gov.cn/gnwkjdt/201007/t20100712_78378.htm.

[50] Nicola Matteucci, The EU State aid policy for broadband: An evaluation of the Italian experience with first generation networks, Telecommunications Policy, Volume 43, Issue 9, 2019, 101830, ISSN 0308-5961.

[51] Harald Gruber, Proposals for a digital industrial policy for Europe, Telecommunications Policy, Volume 43, Issue 2, 2019, Pages 116–127, ISSN 0308-5961, https://doi.org/10.1016/j.telpol.2018.06.003.

explore new ways of investment and financing to activate their economic vitality. While carrying out the above measures, they pay attention to the formulating and improving of relevant policies and regulations. A few countries begin to focus on digital literacy of talents as a significant measure in the digital business environment. The improvement of talents' digital literacy capacity can affect the digital production environment, digital innovation environment and education environment through three paths: improving efficiency, promoting innovation and fostering inclusiveness, thus optimizing the digital business environment and creating a fair, balanced, healthy and sustainable development environment for the digital economy. The above routes have certain significance for the optimizing routes of China's digital business environment as well. China's digital economy ranks in the forefront of the world, and it is extremely urgent to speed up the construction of the overall policy framework and related evaluation indicators of the digital business environment, which could further stay in line with China's basic national conditions. Based on a large number of investigations and studies, the following five key areas are proposed to analyze China's digital business environment.

1. Digital infrastructure, including digital economic foundations such as fixed/mobile broadband, 5G, number of Internet users and digital consumption level, and digital economic supporting systems such as logistics, express delivery, payment and finance.
2. Digital literacy and personnel training, which include digital market innovation and personnel training.
3. Digital government service, the level of digital government service platform, the development of government websites and the development of government new media.
4. Digital regulation, digital opening degree includes admission of foreign investment, digital trade facilitation, attraction of transnational investment, and equal treatment of domestic and foreign enterprises. Digital market order includes market entity in-and- out order, transaction order, competition order and platform autonomy.
5. Digital security. It includes open sharing of government public data, consumer personal data protection, industrial data appreciation, online network trust guarantee order, etc.

Chapter 3
Digital Infrastructure

Abstract At first, this chapter introduces the general situation of China's digital infrastructure construction from three aspects which includes digital infrastructure, digital resource application, and digital access environment. Secondly, it determines the principles for establishing indicators for the evaluation of digital infrastructure and established an evaluation index system for digital infrastructure construction. The system structure mainly includes four first-level indicators, which includes universal network service, postal express service, means of payment, and network security. The four first-level indicators also contain many secondary indicators. Finally, the best practices of China's digital infrastructure construction are introduced: the development of 5G networks, data centers, industrial Internet, basic software, and the digital infrastructure construction practice cases of Baidu Group and Software Park of Haidian District.

Infrastructure is an important symbol of social and economic modernization. In the era of industrial economy, traditional infrastructure is mainly composed of steel bars, cement, masonry, steel structures and other industrial materials. From a visual point of view, these facilities are visible. Traditional infrastructure, as an important support for economic development, plays an obvious role in driving the economy. Especially in the short term, it can expand domestic demand and stimulate economic growth. With China's economy entering a new normal of slowing growth, the marginal benefit of expanding effective investment in traditional infrastructure has declined, and the optimization of industrial structure is limited, which also brings certain government public risks. In the era of digital economy, a complete digital infrastructure is the foundation and guarantee for the development of digital economy, and it is an important support for the realization of high-quality development in China during the 14th Five-Year Plan period.

Digital infrastructure, as its name implies, is the digital infrastructure. Digital infrastructure in a narrow sense refers to the infrastructure based on the evolution and development of the new generation of information technology under the background that data has become the key factor of production. Combing research on new infrastructure, digital infrastructure covers communication network infrastructure

X. Li et al., *Development Practice of Digital Business Environment in China*, Applied Economics and Policy Studies,
https://doi.org/10.1007/978-981-16-8527-9_3

represented by 5G, Internet of Things and Industrial Internet, new technology infrastructure represented by artificial intelligence, cloud computing and blockchain, and data center and intelligent computing center. Represented by digital infrastructure, etc.; Digital infrastructure is not only the infrastructure, but also the infrastructure using advanced technology, which is highly technical and professional and has the general characteristics of infrastructure.

In recent years, China has attached importance to the construction of digital infrastructure, and hereby has held relevant conferences and issued relevant policies to support the development of digital infrastructure. The Central Economic Work Conference in 2018 emphasized the significance to accelerate the pace of 5G to apply in commercial field and strengthen the construction of new infrastructure such as artificial intelligence, industry internet and Internet of Things. In 2019, the government work report of the two sessions (NPC and CPPCC) proposed to strengthen the construction of a new generation of information infrastructure. On February 21, 2020, the Political Bureau of the Central Committee emphasized that the pace of 5G networks and industry internet construction should be accelerated. On March 4, 2020, the Standing Committee of Political Bureau of the Central Committee of the Communist Party of China emphasized that it is necessary to speed up the construction of new infrastructure such as 5G networks and data centers. On April 20, 2020, State Development and Reform Commission first defined the scope of new infrastructure, including information infrastructure, integrated infrastructure and innovative infrastructure. On April 28, 2020, the State Council executive meeting further emphasized accelerating the construction of new infrastructure such as information network (Table 3.1).

3.1 Overview of Digital Infrastructure Construction

Digital infrastructure is a new generation of digital construction, which meets the needs of digital economy development, digital society and digital government, and provides data sensing, collection, storage, transmission, calculation, application and other supporting capabilities. Moreover, data as the important cog fills every part of digital infrastructure machine. Digital infrastructure contains three distinctive levels: network communication level, computing storage level and converged application level. The network communication level includes 4G network, 5G network, optical fiber broadband, IPv6, satellite Internet, etc. The computing storage level includes data center, cloud computing, artificial intelligence, etc. The converged application level includes the general software and hardware infrastructure and digital transformation of traditional infrastructure, all of which can be grouped into industry internet, Internet of Things, basic software, intelligent transportation infrastructure and intelligent energy infrastructure.

Quickening the pace of the construction of digital infrastructure is the optimal combination to effectively stimulate demand and supply in short term and in long run. It is estimated that by the end of 2020, the 5G investment of basic telecom

Table 3.1 Meetings and policies on the deployment of "digital infrastructure"

Date	Meeting/department	Content
December 2018	The Central Economic Working Conference	Strengthen the construction of the Internet of Things and artificial intelligence
May 2019	Executive meeting of the State Council	Combine manufacturing technology with industrial Internet and artificial intelligence
July 2019	Political Bureau Meeting of the CPC Central Committee	Promote the construction of industrial Internet, Internet of Things and information networks
January 2020	Executive meeting of the State Council	Introduce policies related to new infrastructure investment such as the Internet of Things and the Industrial Internet
February 2020	12th meeting of the Central Deep Reform Commission	Overall planning for the coordinated development of traditional and new infrastructure, creating new Capital construction system
March 2020	Standing Committee of Political Bureau of Central Committee	Improve the speed of new infrastructure such as 5G networks and data centers
April 2020	Political Bureau of CPC Central Committee	Transform and upgrade traditional industries, strengthen investment, and expand new infrastructure and strategies Investment in sexual emerging industries
April 2020	Ministry of Transport, National Development and Reform Commission	Integrated development planning of higher quality transportation in the Yangtze River Delta
April 2020	National Development and Reform Commission Central Network Office	Promote the action of "using the cloud to give wisdom" and cultivate the implementation plan of new economic development
April 2020	China Securities Regulatory Commission National Development and Reform Commission	Promote the pilot work of real estate investment trust funds in the infrastructure sector
June 2020	National Development and Reform Commission, etc.	Support private enterprises to participate in the construction and development of transportation infrastructure
July 2020	Political Bureau of CPC Central Committee	Continue to expand domestic demand and accelerate the construction of new infrastructure

(continued)

Table 3.1 (continued)

Date	Meeting/department	Content
July 2020	National development and reform Commission	Accelerate the implementation of the new urbanization construction to complement the shortcomings and strengths, and promote the intelligent transformation of the county
July 2020	National Development and Reform Commission, etc.	Support the healthy development of new formats and new models, activate the consumer market, and promote the expansion of employment
July 2020	National development and reform Commission	Construction of Intercity Railway in Guangdong-Hong Kong-Macao Greater Bay Area
September 2020	National Development and Reform Commission, etc.	Expand investment in strategic emerging industries and foster new economic growth points
October 2020	Fifth Plenary Session of the Nineteenth Central Committee	Accelerate the building of industrial Internet, the fifth generation mobile communication, and the big data center

enterprises will exceed 180 billion yuan. By 2025, 5G will directly create more than 3 million jobs. It is estimated that the scale of China's market will be close to 700 billion yuan in 2020, up 14% year-on-year, and the pace of traditional industries going online and going to the cloud will be accelerated. In the short term, accelerating the construction of digital infrastructure is an effective measure to hedge the impact of the epidemic and the downward pressure on the economy, giving play to the key role of investment, and to realize the "six stabilities" to respond to the call of country. In the long run, critical actions would be taken in such as speeding up the deployment of 5G networks, data centers and cloud computing platforms, and consolidating basic software, promoting the industry internet, and constantly spawning new industrial models and formats such as intelligent transportation, intelligent logistics, telecommuting and online education, so as to stimulate the potential of the digital economy, enhance the national governance capacity, and effectively support the transformation of more digitalized, networked and intelligent economy and society.

In terms of digital infrastructure, as of December 2020, the number of IPv4 addresses in China was 389.23 million, and the number of IPv6 addresses was 57634/32. The total number of domain names in China is 41.98 million. Among them, the total number of domain names labeled ".CN" is 18.97 million, accounting for 45.2% of the total number of domain names in China. The international export broadband is 11,511,397 Mbps, an increase of 30.4% compared with the end of 2019 (Table 3.2).

In terms of digital resource application, as of December 2020, the number of websites in China was 4.43 million, and the number of websites labeled ".CN"

Table 3.2 Comparison of digital basic resources between 2019.12 and 2020.12

Item	December in 2019	December in 2020
IPv4 (number)	387508224	389231616
IPv6 (block/32)	50877	57634
Domain name (number)	50942295	41977611
.CN domain name (number)	22426900	18970054
International export broadband (Mbps)	8,827,751	11,511,397

was 2.95 million. The number of webpages in China is 315.5 billion, an increase of 5.9% compared with the end of 2019, of which the number of static webpages is 215.5 billion, accounting for 68.3% of the total number of webpages, while the number of dynamic webpages is 100 billion, accounting for 31.7% of the total number of webpages. In 2020, the consumption of mobile Internet traffic reached 165.6 billion GB. By December 2020, the number of apps which could be monitored in China's domestic market was 3.45 million, a decrease of 220,000 compared with 2019. The top four apps accounted for 59.2% of the total, and the number of game apps reached 887,000, accounting for 25.7% of the total number of apps. The number of daily tools, e-commerce and life service apps reached 503,000, 340,000 and 310,000 respectively, ranking second and third, accounting for 14.6%, 9.9% and 9.0% of all apps.

In terms of digital access environment, as of December 2020, the proportion of Internet users who use mobile phones in China reached 99.7%, 0.4 percentage points higher than that in March 2020. The proportion of Internet users using desktop computers, laptops, TVs and tablets to surf the Internet is 32.8%, 28.2%, 24.0% and 22.9%, respectively, which are lower than those in March 2020. The average online time of Chinese netizens is 26.2 h per week, which is 4.6 h less than that in March 2019. The number of fixed Internet access users with access rate of 100 Mbps and above accounts for 89.9% of the total number of fixed broadband users. The number of FTTH/O users reached 454 million, accounting for 93.3% of the total fixed Internet broadband access, up 1 percentage compared with the end of 2019. The three basic telecommunications enterprises have developed 1.136 billion cellular Internet of Things end users, an increase of 108 million compared with the end of 2019, among which the end users in intelligent manufacturing, intelligent transportation and intelligent public utilities accounted for 18.5%, 18.3% and 22.1% respectively.

In 2020, the investment in key areas of "new infrastructure" is in full swing, and the systematic project of building a new infrastructure system has been started to meet the needs of modernization in the new stage. In the field of 5G communication, according to the data of the Ministry of Industry and Information Technology, in 2020, more than 600,000 new 5G base stations will be built nationwide, and more than 718,000 5G base stations have been opened. A 5G network covering cities above prefecture level and key counties and cities across the country has been constructed. In the field of industrial Internet, as of January 13, 2021, the high-quality external network of industrial Internet covered more than 300 cities across the country, connecting more than 180,000 industrial enterprises. Five national top-level nodes for industrial Internet logo analysis in Beijing, Guangzhou, Chongqing, Shanghai and Wuhan have been built, covering 34 industries, with a total number of logo registrations reaching 11.14 billion. There are more than 80 industrial Internet platforms with certain industry and regional influence, connecting 60 million sets of industrial equipment and 400,000 industrial enterprises.

3.2 Research on Digital Infrastructure Evaluation Indicator of Digital Business Environment

3.2.1 The Principle of Setting Indicators

Based on the strategic needs of the construction of digital business environment, taking the region as the starting point, there are few researches on the evaluation of digital business environment in the practical situation in China. In view of this condition, based on an in-depth analysis of the evaluation of digital business environment, this report first puts forward a set of evaluation indicators aiming at digital infrastructure, which combines standards and specifications, technology, management, personnel and benefits from various aspects in organic way, and establishes an evaluation model by using tomographic mathematics from simple to complex, which is expected to provide foundation for the sake of decision-making for China's digital business environment.

Overall objective of evaluation indicator system: aiming at promoting the healthy growth of digital business environment construction in China, improving the digitalization level of urban planning, construction, management and service, and promoting the construction of digital and industrial bases in cities, industries and communities, setting a unified, comprehensive and scientific evaluation indicator system for regional digital platform, and forming an indicator system evaluation questionnaire and evaluation manual score table to grade and guide regional informational construction. At the same time, it targets at promoting the simultaneous development of government information construction, enterprise information construction and community information construction.

The design of evaluation indicator should follow the following principles:

(1) Systematic principle

A clear interlocking relationship should be established between each part and level of the indicator system to make it universally representative, so that it can be compared horizontally and evaluated statistically according to the same standard.

(2) Comparability principle

Every indicator in the indicator system is accurate, and the same indicator can be used for comparison in different ranges.

(3) On-juxtaposition principle

In the evaluation process, different weights are given to each indicator, and the main indicator and subordinate indicators cannot be juxtaposed, with primary and secondary importance each.

(4) Singularity principle

Indicators and their expressions and concepts should not be ambiguous, but be scientific, simple and clear, and satisfy the principle of singularity. (i) the interpretation of indicator connotation. Indicators and their expressions should be clear, so that different reviewers might not have different understandings to affect the objectivity of evaluation. (ii) Critical attitude towards indicators. If indicators are treated with different attitudes, the evaluation criteria will be inconsistent.

(5) Compatibility principle

The contents of each indicator cannot be subordinate or deduced from each other, and the characteristics reflected by each indicator should not be repeated or conflicted.

3.2.2 Indicators' Setting

According to the above principles, the previous evaluation indicator research and actual investigation, we established the evaluation indicator system of digital infrastructure construction. The system mainly contains four first-level indicators, namely, universal network service, postal express service, payment means and network guarantee.

(1) The universal network service includes three secondary indicators

   (i) National or urban broadband plans or information infrastructure construction related policies (including universal service funds, preferential loans and subsidies);
   (ii) The popularization rate (%) of fixed broadband and mobile broadband and the average download rate (Mbps);
   (iii) The number of 5G base stations and the number of IPv6 addresses per capita.

(2) The postal express service contains six secondary indicators

   (i) the density of postal service outlets;
   (ii) Online retail sales supported by postal services;
   (iii) The average receiving time of e-commerce logistics express delivery;

(iv) The average charge in every order of postal service;
(v) time and expenses in accordance with of import and export activities;
(vi) Complaints from the market (enterprises and individuals) about postal services;

(3) The means of payment includes four secondary indicators
(i) Whether digital currency is included in pilot and its impact on financial services;
(ii) Digitalization degree of financial institutions;
(iii) The popularity of digital finance;
(iv) Average speed of regional digital payment, including online payment opening, average settlement period, and whether there are transaction barriers between payment service providers.

(4) Network security mainly emphasizes security aspect, including four secondary indicators
(i) The construction of network security-related technological platforms (identifying the construction of related platforms has been started or not, the number and name of platforms, and the technical means and capabilities);
(ii) The occurrence of network security (including data security) incidents (the number and situation of incidents such as computer malicious programs, website security incidents, DDoS attacks, and vulnerability attacks; sensitive data leakage, data abuse, etc.);
(iii) The condition of network security enterprises (the scale of enterprises registered in network security and the scale of employees of this field, etc.);
(iv) The cost of the enterprise to meet the network security requirement (the quantity of approved documents, business costs, time costs).

3.3 Best Practices of Digital Infrastructure Construction in China

3.3.1 5G Network

The fifth generation mobile communication technology (5G for short) is the latest generation of cellular mobile communication technology, which is an extension of 4G, 3G and 2G (GSM) systems. Like the early 2G, 3G and 4G mobile networks, 5G networks are digital cellular networks, and the first generation of mobile communication is analog. One cell and one base station distinguish users with different frequencies, that is, frequency division multiple access. 2G is digital to distinguish users by different time slots, that is, time division multiple access. 3G is CDMA, that is, code division multiple access, which distinguishes users by different code channels. 4G makes use of the three-dimensional factors of frequency, time and code channel, and greatly improves the multiplexing efficiency by orthogonal frequency division multiple access. The multi-access mode of 5G is the evolution of 4G technology, which uses technologies such as large-scale antenna and edge computing. Like previous generations, 5G has been maintained for ten years, and its peak rate has increased by 1000 times in ten years. However, compared with previous generations, 1G to 4G are personal-oriented, and 5G is extended to industrial Internet and smart city applications.

In this network, the service area covered by the provider is divided into many small geographical areas called cells. Analog signals representing sounds and images are digitized in mobile phones, converted by analog-to-digital converters and transmitted as bit streams. The main advantage of 5G network is that the data transmission rate is much higher than that of the previous cellular network, up to 10 gbit/s, faster than the current wired internet and 100 times faster than that of the previous 4GLTE cellular network. Another advantage is lower network delay (faster response time), which is less than 1 ms, while 4G is 30–70 ms.

5G has three major application scenarios, such as enhancing mobile broadband, ultra-reliability, low delay, wide coverage and large connection. Compared with 4G, 5G has one to two orders of magnitude improvement in many performances. The performance of its wireless technology still follows the theory of wireless communication. First, the number of base stations is made more and denser. Secondly, make more antennas, add the use dimension of space division, broaden the available frequencies, and improve the physical layer. Coupled with the network technology, the performance of 5G and 4G has been significantly improved (Fig. 3.1).

In terms of base station construction, as of March 2020, 198,000 5G base stations have been built nationwide, with more than 50 million package users and more than 20 million 5G terminals connected to 56 networks. China Telecom announced that China Unicom and China Telecom is expected to jointly complete the construction of 250,000 5G base stations nationwide in the third quarter of 2020. China Tower company also said it plans to deploy 500,000 towers in 2020. China Mobile strives to achieve 300,000 5G base stations by the end of 2020.

In terms of its application, it is used in HD, 4K/8K, AR/VR, finance, education, security, agriculture, Huoshenshan and Leishenshan hospital, industry internet community and internet of vehicles, etc.

In terms of industrial chain, Huawei, ZTE and Tatfook Technology are key providers of mobile communication infrastructure and key players of base station systems. Eastone Century and Haige Communications Group Incorporation Company plays their roles in network construction. Midstream mobile communication operator services are the three major operators and China Tower. Downstream terminals and application are mobile phones, intelligent home appliances, automobiles and other terminal devices, as well as more application scenes such as Internet of Vehicles, Industry internet, VR/AR, 4K/8K HD video, and telemedicine.

Fig 3.1 Rapid development of 5G

According to *China 5G Economic Report 2020*, the total investment of 5G in China is expected to reach 0.9 trillion yuan in 2020 and 1.5 trillion yuan in 2025, as shown in the table (Table 3.3).

Table 3.3 China's 5G investment in 2020

Name of fund	Target scale (100 million yuan)	Participant
National Integrated Circuit Industry Investment Fund Phase 2	2000	Central Finance, Insurance Investment Fund, China Mobile, China Development Finance, Huaxin Investment
China Mobile 5G Joint Innovation Industry Fund Hunan 5G Internet of Things Industry Fund	300	China Mobile Capital, Guoxin Venture Capital and Chengtong Fund
China Telecom Wisdom Interconnection Industry Fund	150	Hunan Xiangjiang Group and Zhongying Investment
China Unicom 5G Application Innovation Fund	100	China Telecom, China Net Investment, Qianhai Ark
National Integrated Circuit Industry Investment Fund Phase 2	100	China Unicom

3.3.2 Datacenter

Data center is a global cooperative network of specific equipment, which is used to transmit, accelerate, display, calculate and store data and information on the Internet infrastructure. Most electronic components in the data center are driven by low DC power supply. The emergence of data center leads people's understanding from a quantitative and structural world to an uncertain and unstructured world. It will gradually become a part of modern social infrastructure like transportation and network communication, and then have a positive impact on many industries. With the rise of the data center industry, it is more convenient and diversified for netizens to participate in the Internet and contribute content. A huge amount of network data can be stored in the data center. The data value will be higher and higher, and the reliability will be further strengthened (Fig. 3.2).

As the storage and computing infrastructure, the data center, can not only connect with cloud computing and AI, but directly connect with informatization modules such as edge computing and Internet of Things, which is of great significance to national economic and social development and upgrading of information technology industry.

In terms of technical status, digital simulation and modular construction technology are taking center stage of the industry. The new generation of submerged liquid cooling technology is gradually becoming the mainstream cooling technology in the new era of base station. Data Center Infrastructure Management (DCIM) intelligent operation and maintenance technology is gradually replacing the traditional manual operation and maintenance management mode. Now, the data center will develop into a cloud data center. First of all, power supply, cooling and other

Fig 3.2 Busy data center

computer room facilities, in addition, various network resources are needed to realize the virtualization of computing, storage and network. Application is more important in data center, so it is necessary to develop various applications and data center services.

In terms of the industrial chains, the upstream infrastructure is mainly to build various hardware subsystems of the data center. Midstream IDC service main purpose is to provide IDC integration, operation and maintenance services. At present, the mainstay is China Telecom, China Unicom and China Mobile. Downstream terminal users need to store/run content in all walks of life of data center servers which meet the requirement of the emerging information technology industry.

In the past three years, the market size of the data center has grown by about 30%, exceeding 100 billion yuan in 2019. In 2020, the investment in digital centers has increased significantly, and 8 data centers have been built, namely, Kepler Big Data Center Phase II in Foshan and Wusha (Kuanyuan) Big Data Center, Tencent Western Cloud Computing Data Center Phase II and CN Hualu Chongqing Data Lake Industrial Park in Chongqing, Guangdong-Hong Kong-Macao Greater Bay Area Data Center in Guangzhou, Zhangye Cloud Computing Big Data Center; the first phase of China Mobile (Lhasa, Tibet) Data Center in Tibet, Huawei Yunxin Chuangyun Data Center in Hefei.

3.3.3 Industry Internet

Industrial Internet is a result of the integration of global industrial systems with advanced computing, analysis, sensing technology and Internet connection. The essence of industrial internet is to connect and integrate equipment, production lines, factories, suppliers, products and customers closely through an open and global industrial-level network platform, and share various essential resources in the industrial economy efficiently, thereby reducing costs and increasing efficiency through automated and intelligent production methods, helping the manufacturing industry to extend its industrial chain and promoting its transformation and development. Industrial Internet reconstructs global industry, stimulates productivity, and makes the world better, faster, safer, cleaner and more economical by connecting intelligent machines and finally connecting man and machine, combined with software and big data analysis (Fig. 3.3).

The industrial Internet is divided into three parts. The first one is the underlying Internet of Things, which uses the sensor network protocol. The second part is the intranet of the enterprise, using industrial Ethernet or delay-sensitive network. The third part is the industrial Internet platform, which has many computing and processing functions. The intranet and industrial internet platform should be connected to the extranet, which is the internet or the software-defined wide area network. It can be seen that the various parts of the industrial Internet constitute the whole process from data collection and aggregation, transmission and distribution,

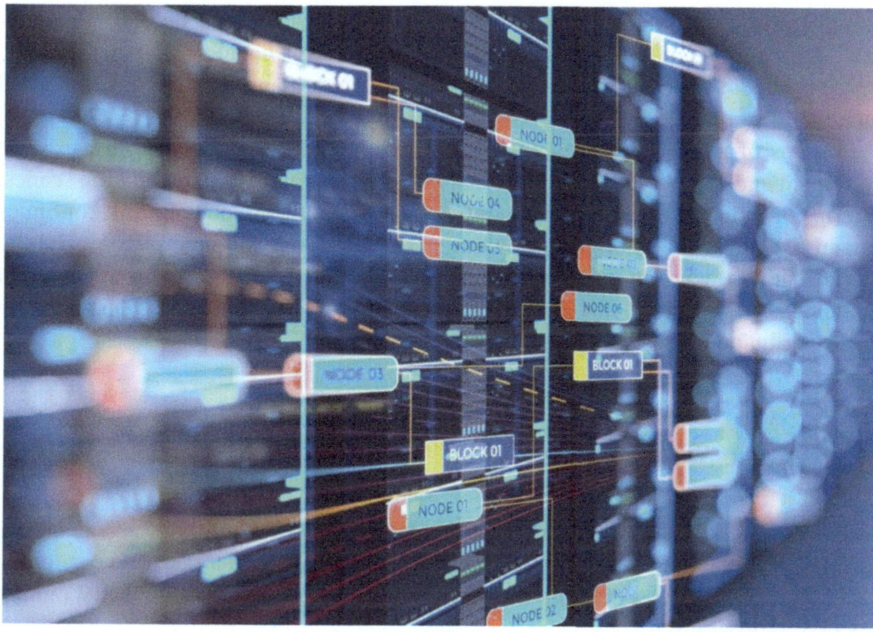

Fig 3.3 All things are connected by industrial Internet

analysis and processing, decision-making and application, and support the data to play the role of production factors.

For the industrial Internet platform, the PaaS layer (platform as a service) in the cloud computing architecture is the first. There are traditional equipment management, resource management, operation and maintenance management, fault management, and big data analysis systems, including artificial intelligence algorithms. The foundation of industrial Internet is SaaS layer (software as a service), and there are various industrial control software, including product life planning, supply chain management, enterprise resource planning, customer relationship management and so on.

In terms of the developments of industry internet: (1) the scale of network coverage continues to expand, and the high-quality external network extends to more than 300 cities across the country. TSN and edge computing are explored and applied in the internal network; (2) The identity resolution system has begun to take shape, with 47 secondary nodes online successfully set and the number of identity registrations exceeding 2.4 billion. The platform connection capability continues to strengthen, and the number of equipment in key platform enterprises connected 690,000 sets. The security capability has been significantly improved, serving more than 90,000 industrial enterprises and 135 platforms.

In terms of application scenes: (1) equipment and production management services, condition monitoring and fault diagnosis, predictive maintenance, remote operation and maintenance, etc. (2) Traditional business and operation optimization, manufacturing optimization, resource scheduling optimization, energy consumption optimization, quality optimization, etc. (3) New models and new formats, digital products, product and service upgrading, on demand manufacturing, shared manufacturing, etc.

In terms of industrial chains, the upper, middle and lower reaches are hardware equipment and software, industry internet platform and industrial application scenes. In terms of industry internet investment, the government's financial input continues to increase. In 2020, among the investment projects have initiated nationwide, the intended investment amount will reach 10 billion yuan. The proportion of social financing keeps rising. In 2019, there were 85 domestic financing cases, and the total disclosed financing amount exceeded 15 billion yuan.

3.3.4 *Basic Software*

Basic software includes operating system, database system, middleware, language processing system (including compiler, interpreter and assembler) and office software (including word processing, spreadsheet, slide show and some elementary picture processing programs).

As the core and basic part of the software industry technology system, basic software is significantly related to national security and economic security, and has always been the focus of technological competition in big-power game. In the trend of technology development, the Internet of Everything (IoE) promotes the development of operating system in the direction of micro-kernel structure; meanwhile, big data and cloud computing prospers distributed database technology.

The industrial chain of basic software mainly contains operating system (Zhongke Fangde, Zhongxing New Pivot, Huawei Hongmeng, etc.), database (Nanda General Motors, Shenzhou General Motors, etc.), middleware (Kingdee Tianyan, Baolande, etc.), office software (Jinshan Office, bid-winning software, etc.), software R&D and testing tools (Industrial Computing Institute of Bank of China, National Software Engineering Center, etc.). It is worth mentioning that in terms of browser kernel, there is no relevant software in China, while the well-known ones abroad are Microsoft, Google, apple, etc.

In terms of investment, the business layout of domestic leading enterprises in the field of basic software has been significantly enhanced. Domestic basic software enterprises continue to strengthen resource integration to form synergies and promote breakthroughs, and foster the ecology of key core technologies. Domestic leading software enterprises seize the opportunity of a new round of technological challenges and increase investment in basic software in emerging fields.

3.3.5 Baidu Group's Digital Infrastructure Practice

Baidu is a leading AI company with a strong Internet foundation. Baidu's vision is to become the world's top high-tech company that understands users best and can help people grow. The word "Baidu" comes from a word of Xin Qiji, a poet in the Southern Song Dynasty, 'The public seeks him thousands of Baidu'. This sentence describes the poet's persistent pursuit of ideals. At the end of 1999, Li Yanhong, who was in Silicon Valley of the United States, saw the great development potential of Chinese Internet and Chinese search engine services, and held the dream of technology changing the world. He founded Baidu Company in Zhongguancun on January 1, 2000.

Baidu has tens of thousands of engineers, which is the top technical team in China and even in the world. This team has mastered the most advanced search engine technology in the world, making Baidu a Chinese high-tech enterprise that has mastered the world's cutting-edge scientific core technology, and making China one of the only four countries in the world with search engine core technology besides the United States, Russia and South Korea.

In 2020, the global economy will be at risk because of the global spread of COVID-19 epidemic. Facing the downward pressure of the global economy, China proposes to increase the construction of new infrastructure to release the vitality of economic growth. Under the new infrastructure strategy, science and technology enterprises, as the main force of digital new infrastructure, have adjusted their strategies one after another. In June, 2020, Baidu made a big move in adding new infrastructure. Following the recent announcement of the industry's first AI new infrastructure map, Baidu released a grand blueprint for new infrastructure investment in the next 10 years, increasing investment in new infrastructure fields such as artificial intelligence, chips, cloud computing and data centers, among which the scale of cloud servers was expanded by 5 million units, and then 5 million AI talents were trained for the society.

Whether e-commerce online shopping could play an important role continuously, and whether there are relevant policies to support model "internet+" to keep on creating another brand-new model. With the formal implementation of the regulations on optimizing the business environment, China is expected to increase policy support for data, to strive to build China's own business force, and to create new opportunities for the development of digital economy in private economy.

Baidu actually has some simple reflection. First, it expects to support private enterprises to participate in new infrastructure construction, new consumption and new service innovation. In particular, Beijing has issued a series of policy support after its operation, and its economy is developing at a high speed. With a series objective on accelerating the pace of cultivating and expanding new business forms and developing sharing economy and intelligent economy have been stated, so some suggestions are put forward: Is it possible to appropriately loosen the restrictions on private enterprises participating in some new building material projects, for example, private enterprises are allowed to purchase the shares through the mixed-ownership reform and enter the new building material field.

The second aspect is to support private enterprises to participate in the new consumption of institutional economy, such as the layout of Internet hospitals.

The third aspect is to encourage private enterprises to expand new services of digital economy, participate in the construction of intelligent cities, and support private enterprises to develop blockchain-related services. The prime purpose is to strengthen the research on basic core technologies, include industrial chain of photoelectric technology in the national key research and development plan of the 14th Five-Year Plan and major national science and technology projects, speed up the research on the obstacles faced by core technologies and products, strengthen the ability of building artificial intelligence, and encourage the development of open-source platforms and deep learning platforms. For example, Baidu has promoted its own technology platform, such as AI chips and AI computing in the Internet of Things. At the same time, it pays attention to the long-term support for basic core technologies and following local regulations. The second purpose is to acquire knowledge in area of basic core technologies application, which is a typical practice. Encouraging enterprises to innovate applications demonstrates the critical role of 5g and artificial intelligence, and providing a favorable foundation for technological innovation and product application periphery. Baidu has also carried out relevant tests in traditional areas of Yizhuang, and up to now, great achievements have already been obtained. Thirdly, Baidu expects to optimize an environment for the development of new technologies and new formats in order to accelerate the pace of innovation followed by policies.

3.3.6 Construction of Software Park in Haidian District

Zhongguancun Software Park covers an area of 139 ha, with a total construction area of over 600,000 m^2, a floor area ratio of 0.44 and an average of 3 floors. The park consists of a business district and a natural district. The business district is located on the east and south sides of the park. The architectural layout is arranged in the form of blocks, and the buildings are connected with each other by garden green space. Incubators, public technical support systems, information centers, talent training centers and hotels in this area have been built and used. The international convention and exhibition center and stadiums will soon be completed and put into use. By the end of 2018, there were nearly 700 enterprises in Zhongguancun Software Park, including 67 listed companies and 71 enterprises with revenues exceeding 100 million yuan, with total revenues exceeding 250 billion yuan and output value of 96.9 billion yuan per square kilometer.

More than a decade ago, Haidian District, as the earliest national software industrial base and export base, carried out software R&D and software export. Now, followed the lead by national digital service organization, Haidian District is expected to do the business service related the digital economy. The whole park covers an area of more than 20 km^2, and the whole area has strict physical planning for the sake of the superior authorities included. Therefore, in the future, it is necessary to do network security monitoring, and some personnel logistics information monitoring in relative clear monitoring range.

By the end of last year, the output value of the whole park was 280 billion yuan, and the output value per square kilometer exceeded 110 billion yuan, which is said to have exceeded one financial street, but it was also affected by Covid-19, resulting the industry growing against the trend. This year it made an outstanding performance with excellent gathering strength of the whole staff, and its whole output value and the number of intellectual property rights took also leading in the whole country. Additionally, it is also assured a place in the world stage. The whole park seems like artificial intelligence blockchain by means of powerful cooperation, while some enterprises are engaged with quantum science and technology and the Internet, so these enterprises are inherently international. Kwai, for example, it is seen as a new media incorporation but in fact, it runs as an artificial intelligence enterprise essentially. It buys and sells the world to do business, so we also help these enterprises to do global service layout. These are some real case of enterprises' development.

There are about 700 enterprises in park, which are divided into major factions. The primary one is Baidu group and Lenovo group. The enterprises in these two groups basically cover 80% of the enterprises in the park. The enterprises in the group no matter what is the name, for example, Pactera incorporation, in fact, are owned and invested by Lenovo, or it is for Lenovo to do OEM work. They become the partner of 157 Fortune Global 50 companies under the context of digital transformation, whose digital services cover high-tech, finance, manufacturing, telecommunications, Internet, automobile, education and many other areas. In addition, like Baidu, as these two group enterprises are old-fashioned enterprises in Haidian District of Beijing, these years have witness the rapid growth of some of them. One is Xiaomi and another is Tencent. However foreign capital invested companies is relatively feeble here. As we all know, IBM R&D Center has issued relevant notices that its core software has been withdrawn mainland, so there is one question for Haidian Park to consider: the remaining employee's problems. Haidian Software Park took more than a month to make the best use of these 700 people, including hunting jobs up to Tencent, finding a job in the five biggest banks in China as a data analysist, or awaiting job assignment, all of which are considered as an acceptable move. On the other hand, with the overall aim at fastening their pace in information technology in new generation, some enterprises began to produce the digital content as they grow faster than ever. In fact, in the past, software enterprises were more of a backstage as a tool to acquire knowledge, but now they are more of a front desk to showcase their content, such as Tencent project, Sina, and Kwai all of which are all content-oriented.

Chapter 4
Digital Order

Abstract This chapter first clarifies the concept of digital market order, which starts from the concept of order to the concept of market order, and then leads to the new concept and connotation of digital market order. Then we studied the evaluation indicators of the digital market order, including 3 secondary indicators, 10 tertiary indicators, and 27 four-hierarchy indicators. Finally, it introduces the best practice cases of China's digital business environment, including Alibaba anti-counterfeiting alliance, Alibaba's anti-monopoly investigation, and a case of using live broadcast e-commerce platform to maintain market order, etc.

4.1 Concepts and Development of Digital Market Order

4.1.1 Concepts of Market Order

Order refers to the state in which the parts or elements that make up a thing are arranged or connected in a natural, orderly, and harmonious way. Market order refers to the standardization of market subjects and objects in the market economy and the recognition and compliance of various subjects with the rules and customs of the market economy in their business activities. The market order in a narrow sense only includes the order of market subjects and objects and the standardization of market transaction behavior. In a broader sense, it also consists of the order maintainers' activity status and effect. However, market order in its broadest sense takes the whole economic operation mechanism and operation order into account, covering all objects in the study of economics. The analysis in this Chapter centers on the evaluation system of market order in the narrow sense, but it does not exclude the discussion in a broader sense in further research.

"Order," being relative to "rules," refers to the degree of conformity between the state, behavior, position and function of the object regulated by the rules and what the rules require. There are rules of an institutional nature, which are manifested in various written laws, regulations and rules, etc.; of a social nature, which are displayed in standard practices accepted and followed by most economic entities; and of a financial nature, which are demonstrated in the requirement of economic

X. Li et al., *Development Practice of Digital Business Environment in China*, Applied Economics and Policy Studies,
https://doi.org/10.1007/978-981-16-8527-9_4

laws on economic entity. It is worth noting that these rules are at different levels. Among them, the rule of the economy is the foundation. For instance, the law of value always plays its role spontaneously and "natural order" is thus formed through the manipulation of the "invisible hand." The social rules, on the one hand, embody the public's sense of the objective rules; on the other hand, they integrate the public's understanding of fairness and justice. Such kind of rules formed in the long-term practice serves as a bridge between economic and institutional rules. Institutional rules, which are at the top level, refer to the authority's affirmation with those public-recognized practices and are presented in the form of laws and regulations, so they are mandatory. Meanwhile, since institutional rules are also the affirmation, limitation, or supplementation of laws by the legislature or the government based on the comprehensive understanding of various laws, they must serve specific social purposes. Therefore, it is inevitable that these rules may conflict with the laws in a particular field. When such contradictions do occur to the extent that they impede the regular operation of activities in that field, a re-examination of the rationality of the rules themselves becomes necessary.

It follows that rules of economic nature, as a research object of economics, cannot be used as a basis for evaluating the market order due to its spontaneity and people's knowledge. Social rules which integrate people's value orientation picture an ideal state of order; but on the other hand, they are not compulsory for all to follow so that they can be used as a basis for order evaluation, but not as the main one. In contrast, although institutional rules may contradict the laws in some particular fields, with their comprehensive feature, universal binding effect, complete mechanism of action, and most comprehensive social recognition, they naturally come first as the primary indicator for market order evaluation. In addition to the existing laws and regulations, ethical norms such as business integrity should also be involved in the evaluation system.

The market order evaluation system comprises a set of interrelated indicators which reflect the degree of conformity between the operation of market elements and the relevant laws and regulations and the practices recognized by the majority of the public from the perspective of microeconomic activities. By using such a system, we can make a qualitative evaluation and measure the degree of market operation, detect problems existing in market operation and provide insights and guidance for the order maintainers.

A country's market is an extensive system, consisting of numerous segmented markets, each with its unique characteristics. However, there is also market identity in various markets: their essence is trading relationship. Accordingly, the market order evaluation system is divided into two levels, one is for the identity of multiple markets, or the comprehensive evaluation of the market; the other is for the particularity of each specific segmented market. Besides, the content of the market order evaluation system can vary with the market structure and its region. That is to say, an optimum evaluation system of market order should include a series of indicators with different levels and ranges that are both interrelated and different.

David Weinberger proposes the concepts of "the three orders of order" in his book *Everything Is Miscellaneous: The Power of the New Digital Disorder*. He divides the order into three order organizations. "In the first order of order, we organize things themselves," which means that things are arranged in a linear order, and each has a fixed position in physical space according to a certain logic. In the second-order of order, information is separated from things, but there are still linked by some kind of pointing. Data becomes an object agent of the first-order organization and points to the physical location of the object by some encoding method. However, the third order is a new one formed in the digital era. "Content is digitalized into bits, and the information about that content consists of bits as well." Each thing constitutes metadata, which is linked and independent of each other, forming a new digital order of "disorder."

4.1.2 Development of Digital Market Order Theory

Attaching great importance to digital development, China has launched "Digital China Initiative." The Fifth Plenary Session of the 19th CPC Central Committee opened in October 2020 has passed The Recommendations of the Central Committee of the Communist Party of China for the 14th Five-year Plan for Economic and Social Development and the Long-range Goals Through 2035, which proposed to "accelerate digital development" and made systematic deployment in this regard. Digital economy, digital society, and digital government are the crucial parts of digital development, mutually supportive, interpenetrating and intertwined. At present, industries of China's digital economy are at different stages of development. Industry 4.0 and new retail are still in their infancy, while sectors such as online video, online marketing, and online shopping have entered a mature stage.

Digital technology has served as an essential driving force in social development today, and it has given rise to "digital culture" in this age, which refers to cultural forms, connotations and traditions in digital formats, as well as related habits and ways of thinking. However, the development of digital technology is now plagued by the following problems: (i) data quality, (ii) "data sharing," and (iii) "lack of knowledge."

The problems mentioned above illustrate a chaotic situation in today's digital world. To develop a digital economy, an excellent digital order is indispensable. But what is digital order? "Order" in this context means regularity and its performance. Digital order is the regularity and interpretation of the existence, development and evolution of the digital world. It includes digital theory and digital technology. They interact with each other and depend on each other, and cannot be separated.

First of all, theoretically speaking, digital earth is a digital mapping from the real world (including nature and human society) to the digital world. The digital order is a digital mechanism function of natural ecological laws and socio-economic laws (generally referring to the economic effects of human social development laws, among which economic laws are the main ones).

Second, technically speaking, digital order refers to the integration mechanism of various digital technologies to build digital earth. Digital technology here refers to software technology, hardware technology, and network technology, etc.

China has established an access management system that encompasses various new models, new business forms and covers both online and offline business. The system sets precise requirements on the business entities, practitioners, product services, business practices in the digital economy, which has been playing an essential role in regulating competitive behavior, preventing potential risks, and safeguarding the rights and interests of users. However, there also exist many problems in market access, such as excessive affairs, high qualification and red tapes. Besides, regional management, multi-regulation, and unclear requirements have further increased the difficulty of licensing, which conflicts with many features of the digital economy such as cross-industry integration, cross-regional operations and rapid iteration. As for the first three predicaments, measures should be taken to ease market access in the digital economy: accelerating the multi-sectoral joint inspection and testing on mobile applications (APP) to avoid repeated detection and simplifying the market access in online car-hailing industry.

Fairness, transparency and even liquidity have been a natural existence in traditional financial markets, and have also undoubtedly become the prerequisites for any market or any trade. However, this is not the case for the digital asset market. Despite the growing regulation on cryptocurrencies, which we are willing to see, it is still the exchange operators leading the way in this field. We need to draw on the experience of market regulation; for another, we need to take the characteristics of the blockchain into account so we can make targeted measures for the cryptocurrency market. Some key elements, we believe, should involve thorough identification procedures, specialized market regulation, consensus-building rules, appropriate infrastructure, and marketing training. On December 25, 2018, China Market Regulation Roundtable was held in Beijing, the theme of which was "fair competition and antitrust in the era of digital economy." Seventeen experts and scholars have provided their profound insights and constructive suggestions based on the current issues concerning fair competition and anti-monopoly, namely, the regulation and governance of cross-border competition in the Internet era, deliberation on the relationship between policies of competition and high-tech industry development in digital economy age, competition neutrality and fair competition review in the "new normal" era and competition policy in the context of intellectual property rights.

On February 7, 2021, the Antitrust Committee of the State Council released The Antitrust Guidelines of the Anti-Monopoly Committee of the State Council on Platform Economy, emphasizing that the Anti-Monopoly Law and supporting regulations and rules apply to all industries and treat all types of market players fairly and impartially. This provides effective and targeted institutional rules for anti-monopoly regulation in the platform economy. It will help antitrust agencies to set enforcement standards and increase enforcement transparency, and deepen market players' understanding of The Anti-Monopoly Law in order to prevent and stop monopolistic acts in the platform economy and promote the development of the platform economy.

4.2 Digital Business Environment–Research on Evaluation Indicators of Digital Market Order

According to the characteristics of market activities and the requirements of "to establish a good order for market-entry, market competition, and market transaction, ensure fair trade, equal competition and the legitimate rights and interests of operators and consumers" as proposed in the Decision of the Central Committee of the Communist Party of China on Several Issues Concerning the Establishment of Socialist Market Economy System, the market order can be assessed by four categories of indicators, namely, indicators of market entry and exit, transaction, competition, and online network trust guarantee.

Market entry and exit order indicators include two sub-categories, namely, subject access and exit order and object entry and exit order, which are used to evaluate the qualifications and conditions of market subjects and the entry and exit status of market subjects and objects. The market subject is the actor of market transaction activities. For its evaluation, the key is to identify whether it is well-conditioned for business activities and whether it meets the qualifications required by the relevant laws and regulations. In other words, this indicator evaluates whether market subjects have the human and capital conditions for their activities, as well as whether they have been granted business qualifications in accordance with the regulations, and whether they have been registered and qualified to operate in accordance with the law. The physical market is the bearer of trading activities and the carrier of the market. Instead of directly engaging in commodity trade, it provides services for commodity trading activities. Therefore, it is a special kind of subject. Its evaluation is similar to that of ordinary subjects, i.e., the conditions and qualifications should also be evaluated, but the content has unique characteristics, and the selection of indicators must reflect such exceptionality. The market intermediary is an intermediary organizer of trading activities, which is not directly engaged in the commodity business, but serves commodity operators. Therefore, it is also a particular type of market subject and its evaluation must focus on qualifications. The market object refers to the goods (including services) that are traded on the market. The evaluation of the market object is still essentially evaluating of the operator's primary behavior through the market object. The assessment of the market object includes whether they are legally prohibited in the market, whether the goods with special requirements comply with the relevant conditions, and whether the goods with only general provisions in the law meet the minimum national standards, etc.

The indicators of market transaction order utilize operator-consumer relation and operator-operator relation to evaluate various transaction relations. The relationship between the operator and the consumer is mainly reflected in whether consumers' nine rights are respected and maintained, with special emphasis put on the volume of consumer complaints and whether these complaints are handled in a timely and reasonable manner. The relationship between the operators is mainly reflected in whether the transaction is conducted following the principle of faith and fairness as well as the conclusion and performance of the contract between the two parties, with particular emphasis on the performance of the contract.

Indicators of market competition order include two sub-categories of unfair competition indicators and indicators of obstructive and restrictive behaviors of competition, used to evaluate competition relations among operators. Dishonest competition behaviors include the infringement of other operators' legitimate rights and interests and the act of gaining competitive advantage by illegal means. The prevention and restriction of competition include the actions of powerful operators crowding out competitors by improper means and the acts of other organizations abusing their power to restrict competition.

Indicators of online network trust guarantee order include telecom network fraud governance and its effectiveness, online intellectual property protection, user data privacy protection, and administration of business practices within the platform.

According to the above guidelines, specific indicators of the market order evaluation system can be designed as follows.

The digital market order contains three two-tier indicators, ten three-tier indicators, and 27 four-tier indicators.

(1) Indicators of market entry and exit

  (i) Indicators of market subject's entry and exit: (a) entry and exit of operators: operator's acceptance rate, license rate; (b) entry and exit of intermediary: market intermediary qualification and acceptance rate, the withdrawal rate of unqualified market intermediaries; (c) entry and exit of market carriers: market carrier qualification and acceptance rate, qualification rate of procedure establishment, the exit rate of unqualified market carriers.

  (ii) Indicators of market object's entry and exit: (a) legally prohibited items case index; (b) restricted goods: violation case or value index, the incidence rate of significant cases; (c) goods of free circulation: product qualification rate, identification rate.

(2) Indicators of transaction order

  (i) Indicators of operator-to-consumer transaction relation: (a) accurate pricing rate; (b) consumer complaints rete; (c) incidence rate of infringement of consumer's rights.

  (ii) Indicators of operator-to-operator relation: (a) contract signing rate; (b) contract compliance rate; (c) invalid contract rate; (d) illegal contract rate; (e) economic contract dispute case index.

(3) Indicators of competition order

  (i) Indicators of unfair competition: (a) counterfeit registered trademark and business case index; (b) infringement of trade secrets case index; (c) damage to competitors' business reputation case index; (d) counterfeit or fraudulent use of quality marks, falsification of origin, false quality representation of goods case index; (e) commercial bribery case index;

(f) false advertising case index (false advertising rate); (g) illegal sales with prizes case index; (h) incidence rate of significant cases of unfair competition (i) other major criminal cases index.

(ii) Indicators of impeding and restricting competition: (a) low price dumping case index; (b) behavior of impeding and restricting competition case index; (c) abuse of administrative power to restrict fair competition case index; (d) incidence of significant cases of impeding and restricting competition.

(4) Indicators of online network trust guarantee order

(i) Cyber fraud countermeasures; (a) Cyber fraud control; (b) Effect of cyber fraud control.
(ii) Online intellectual property protection; (a) Intellectual property protection measures; (b) Effect of intellectual property protection.
(iii) Supervision of the collection and use of user data by enterprises.
(iv) Governance of business practices within the platform: (a) Network commodity quality supervision; (b) False advertising; (c) Food safety.

4.3 Best Practice of Digital Market Order

4.3.1 Alibaba Anti-counterfeiting Alliance

Zheng Junfang, chief platform governance officer of Alibaba Group, said that as trying its best to take on its responsibilities, Ali had given full play to the role of the Internet and digital technology, taking the initiative to collaborate with the government to bring together consumers, businesses, rights holders and partners to provide infrastructure and solutions for social governance.

Taking the social governance of intellectual property as an example, in January 2017, Alibaba Anti-counterfeiting Alliance (AACA) was established. This alliance launched by Alibaba and jointly built by many domestic and overseas brands like Apple and Louis Vuitton cooperates with law enforcement agencies. Currently, more than 110 brands from 16 countries around the world have joined AACA, among which 84 are foreign brands, accounting for 76%.

The anti-counterfeiting co-governance system of "law enforcement agency plus brand rights holder plus Ali platform" developed by AACA not only focuses on combating online fakes but also mobilizes social efforts to help brands trace the source of offline fakes. It manages to do what brands couldn't, contributing its solutions to tackle infringement and counterfeiting, and making it possible to "combat fakes like controlling drunk driving."

Statistics show that from April 1 to September 5 this year, AACA has provided nearly 200 clues of fake selling to the national public security organs, helping to smash 214 mills and arrest 620 suspects, with a total of 2.88 billion yuan involved.

According to the Report on the Latest Development of IPR Protection and Business Environment in China (2017), Alibaba has united leading domestic and foreign brands to establish a big data anti-counterfeiting alliance. With the information it collected, law enforcement departments have carried out interprovincial (district or municipal) action, safeguarding the legitimate rights and interests of a number of Chinese and foreign brand owners such as Apple, Chanel and Sony.

IPR protection is just like business creation, empowering Ali's brand and business to create more value. Leading brands including McDonald's, General Motors, COFCO, Baili, Jahwa and TRULIVA have joined AACA before November 11, 2018, and nearly 40 of the AACA brand members have joined "Tmall Double 11's Billionaire Club" in 2018. Insiders said that the continuous expansion of membership and the prosperous business performance of the brand had made AACA one of the most influential anti-counterfeiting alliances in the world.

4.3.2 Alibaba Under Antitrust Investigation

In December 2020, China's General Administration of Market Supervision, based on the report and prior verification, initiated an investigation into suspected monopolistic behaviors such as "Exclusive Choosing" against Alibaba Group Holding Limited.

(1) The legal investigation of Internet enterprises suspected of monopolistic behavior such as "Exclusive Choosing" is a concrete manifestation of strengthening anti-monopoly in the platform economy.

This shows that the internet industry is not outside the law. The Anti-Monopoly Law applies to all entities, whether they are domestic-funded or foreign-funded enterprises, state-owned enterprises or private enterprises, internet enterprises or traditional enterprises. All entities are treated equally before the Anti-Monopoly Law. Over the past 12 years since the implementation of the Anti-Monopoly Law, China has carried out anti-monopoly enforcement in various industries. There is no denying that competition in the Internet industry is distinctly different from that of traditional industries. For example, the business model with the Internet as the carrier itself is the product of information and communication technology innovation and is still in continuous innovation. The competition is dynamic and the effect is multilateral. Therefore, Western jurisdictions have gone through the necessary "wait and see" phase of antitrust enforcement in the Internet industry. As far as China is concerned, the supervision of the Internet industry adheres to the principle of "inclusiveness and prudence," to maintain competition, encourage innovation and promote high-quality economic development. It is not to allow unfair competition or restrict competition in the Internet industry. For this reason, the legal investigation into the suspected monopolistic behavior of Alibaba Group should not be interpreted as special law enforcement against the Internet field, but rather as a concrete manifestation of the normalization of anti-monopoly law enforcement, and should not be construed as a denial of innovation, a denial of the Internet economy or a rejection of the platform business model.

This investigation by the General Administration of Market Supervision on Internet enterprises suspected of monopolistic behavior, such as "Exclusive Choosing," is a concrete manifestation of strengthening anti-monopoly in the platform economy. The platform economy has a complex business model and balance of interests. Through professional anti-monopoly law enforcement and perfect procedures, it can protect fair competition and consumer welfare in the platform economy field, but also help to improve China's anti-monopoly law enforcement system, enhance law enforcement effectiveness, and promote the construction of a high-level socialist market economy system.

The investigation into Alibaba's suspected monopoly by the General Administration of Market Supervision is a regular anti-monopoly law enforcement action with milestone significance, because a good order of competition in the Internet marketer needs to be maintained with the joint efforts of the government, regulators, platform companies, and consumers, each in their way. With the rapid development of the online economy, many problems such as monopoly, unfair competition have emerged. In this phase, it is necessary to examine and eliminate the behaviors that endanger competition and innovation so that the online economy can achieve sound development. This antitrust investigation is not carried for cracking down on an enterprise or suppressing the innovation and development of the industry, but for the purpose of better regulating and developing the online economy, putting a "bridle" on the "wild horse" of the online economy, and enabling the internet industry to move forward on the track of the rule of law.

(2) The investigation into the "Exclusive Choosing" and other suspected monopolistic behaviors will facilitate the standardization and development of the platform economy.

In recent years, Internet platforms have continuously improved market concentration by their advantages in data, technology and capital. Meanwhile, market resources have accelerated to cluster with leading platform enterprises, and the problem of internet platform monopoly has begun to emerge. From the point of view of competition damage, platform enterprises with dominant market position have no justifiable reason to adopt "Exclusive Choosing" and other restrictive transactions, which will not only limit the trading options of merchants and consumers, but also potentially exclude the restriction of competition in relevant markets, inhibit innovation and harm the interests of consumers. According to the law, the market supervision department will initiate a case investigation against the internet enterprises suspected of monopolistic behavior, which will play a positive role in standardizing and developing the platform economy and guiding and promoting its healthy development. After the anti-monopoly investigation procedure starts, the follow-up investigation will be carried out according to the evidence obtained from the legal inquiry.

Strengthening the anti-monopoly law enforcement is necessary to fortify the anti-monopoly and improve the socialist economic system. It is also required for the regulatory authorities to enhance the enforcement of law on suspected monopolistic behaviors such as "Exclusive Choosing" in the Internet field. It is in line with the purpose of the Anti-Monopoly Law to safeguard fair competition order and protect consumers' interests through the investigation and handling of cases. If it is found that the "Exclusive Choosing" behavior violates the Anti-Monopoly Law, the operator will face a hefty fine. The legal responsibility to stop the illegal acts will have the effect of reshaping the business model of the operators, and the market competition damage will thus be relieved accordingly.

The "Exclusive Choosing" behavior involved in this investigation is also known as restricted trading. The investigation of internet companies suspected of monopolistic behavior by the regulatory authorities is just a start. It is complicated to identify whether the parties in the case are involved in "Exclusive Choosing": the first step is to judge whether the parties have a dominant position in the market and whether their behaviors have the consequences of restricting or harming competition. It also needs to go through a series of procedures such as an investigation by the law enforcement authorities, fixed evidence and expert argumentation. Simultaneously, once the market participants involved in the case are identified as conducting monopolistic behavior, they will be punished with a high penalty of 1–10% of the turnover. It is believed that this regulatory authority's investigation is the result of great deliberation.

(3) Strengthening anti-monopoly supervision is an inevitable requirement for creating a new development pattern, building a high-level socialist market economic system and comprehensively promoting reform and opening up.

In recent years, China's Internet economy has been booming, with new forms and models emerging one after another, and competition has been getting fierce. This investigation will definitely encourage internet companies to give priority to legal competition and create a more conducive environment for digital economy.

The implementation of the Anti-Monopoly Law in the Internet industry facilitates both competition and innovation in the Internet industry. Maintaining competition and encouraging innovation are two sides of the same coin. If we want to provide fertile soil for innovation, we must keep a good market competition order; if we are going to get rid of low-level competition and improve the strength of competition, we must encourage innovation. Only by maintaining competition and encouraging innovation, can the Internet industry act as a driver for higher economic efficiency, better economic structure, consumer welfare, and economic growth.

4.3.3 E-commerce Livestreaming Platforms Help to Maintain Market Order and Create New Governance Models

Live broadcast refers to a kind of network activity that uses Internet communication technologies such as video and audio to display related products, contents and services and interact with users instantly. As a new tool, live broadcast can be organically combined with various industrial forms. Compared with traditional offline business activities, e-commerce completes transactions and related service activities on the Internet in an electronic way, and all links of e-commerce have changed, moving towards electronic and networked development.

This form of "live broadcast + e-commerce" makes live broadcast e-commerce and e-commerce live broadcast develop and promote each other. The anchor can introduce the situation of various commodities in real time, display them, and finally launch sales promotion through visual live broadcast. In this process, instant video plays a very important role, and the anchor communicates and interacts with consumers, playing the role of offline shopping guide, and finally reaching a deal. It can be seen that the essence of live e-commerce is still e-commerce, but it is a new type of retail activity, which realizes stable realization of traffic by shortening the supply chain. Live broadcast visualizes e-commerce shops and enables the anchor and fans to interact online in real time, thus subverting the traditional planar commodity advertising mode, and consumers can perceive commodities in all directions in real time.

As livestream selling industry is developing in full swing, it plays an important role in activating the consumer market, promoting employment and promoting economic development. Against this backdrop, cities including Guangzhou, Hangzhou, Chengdu, Chongqing, Jinan, Yiwu have issued policies to seize the heights of the live e-commerce industry.

From the central policy level, 2016 is the beginning year of live broadcast. With the gradual popularization of the Internet, the number of netizens watching live broadcast is increasing. At the same time, with the development of entertainment industry as the background, most people in China think that live broadcast has a good development prospect. For a time, live broadcast platforms have mushroomed, which also promotes the rapid development of live broadcast e-commerce in the future. With the rapid development, the regulatory loopholes in the live broadcast industry have also been exploited by many people. Many anchors have adopted a variety of bottomless opportunistic behaviors to attract powder and collect wealth, such as the "live broadcast" scandal in early 2016, and such incidents have produced very serious consequences. The state issued a large number of policies to supervise the live broadcast industry in 2016, and the attitude of the state functional regulatory authorities to live webcasts has also changed from passive acceptance to active supervision, a series of policy norms.

In 2016, Beijing Network Culture Association, together with more than 20 enterprises involved in webcasting, promoted the signing of a self-discipline convention in the field of webcasting. The convention stipulated the watermark standard for webcasting rooms, requiring the storage of live videos, the need for the anchors to provide ID card information registration, the establishment of a list of anchor records with violations, and the real-time supervision by special personnel in each live room. In June of the same year, the code of conduct for live webcasting marketing was issued, which was the first document to make relevant regulations on live webcasting. A month later, in order to regulate the network performance behavior, the Ministry of Culture issued a notice to manage the network performance communication behavior.

In September 2016, the State Administration of Radio, Film and Television put forward new requirements for the live broadcast platform, requiring the live broadcast platform to obtain relevant certificates before going online. At the same time, in order to strengthen the management of webcasting services, it is expressly stipulated that any subject is prohibited from using the names of TV stations and radio stations for publicity activities without official authorization. The release of this document marks that the webcasting industry is officially supervised by the State Administration of Radio, Film and Television. However, the above documents did not explain the live broadcast qualification, and did not further define the scope of the relevant content on the live broadcast platform. The most important point is to improve the construction of the anchor credit system. Considering these shortcomings, the Central Network Office issued the live broadcast management regulations to standardize the above deficiencies in a documentary manner.

The Internet belongs to a place within the law, and the state has gradually strengthened the management of Internet live broadcast since 2018. For example, in 2018, 12 online performance platforms were forcibly stopped by the Ministry of Culture, and the content violations of more than 30 platforms were investigated and dealt with. After that, six departments, led by the Ministry of Industry and Information Technology, jointly issued documents to further standardize the related issues of live broadcast service, which put forward new requirements for the live broadcast platform. The platform must require the use of user real-name registration system, and strengthen the management of anchors and live broadcast content. Therefore, the major live broadcast platforms began to carry out content supervision, and the resulting high operating costs led to the increase of industry barriers, and many small and medium-sized platforms were unable to make ends meet and faced with crisis.

During the epidemic in 2020, live e-commerce has experienced explosive growth. After the epidemic control, in order to ensure the healthy development of live e-commerce, on the one hand, relevant departments have given answers on how to evaluate online marketing integrity. On the other hand, it regulates the basic requirements for the operation and service of live broadcast e-commerce. It is worth mentioning that the application scope of these two documents is nationwide. After that, the Advertising Association promulgated the live webcast marketing standard and began to implement it, standardizing the live webcast marketing activities. The main body coverage of the standard content includes consumers, marketing anchors, merchants, live broadcast platforms, MCN institutions, etc. The documents are based on the basic principles that marketing activities should abide by, and then separate specifications and classified incentives are carried out according to different specific subjects, prohibiting online marketing live broadcast data fraud, such as modifying and falsifying transaction and user evaluation data. Live broadcast propaganda should seek truth from facts, and should not exaggerate the product effect or lead to misunderstanding. In addition, the code encourages all subjects to actively conduct public welfare live broadcasts to help the country get rid of poverty and revitalize the countryside.

In order to rectify the chaos in the live broadcast e-commerce industry, to convey to the public the signal that the Internet is not an extra-legal place, and to show the government's determination to promote the healthy and sustainable development of the live broadcast e-commerce, the Central Network Information Office and seven departments have carried out special rectification and standardized management of the live broadcast e-commerce, which lasted for half a year. In the future, the above departments will explore the classification rules of live webcasts and clarify the rules of goods management.

According to incomplete statistics, as of June 2020, more than 10 cities have issued support policies related to e-commerce live broadcast. Some cities with better economic development, such as Beijing, Shanghai and Guangzhou, have issued relevant laws and regulations to support the development of e-commerce live broadcast, as shown in Table 4.1.[1]

(1) Alibaba Group—Taobao livestreaming platform

Taobao livestreaming platform refuses the viewer rewards and beauty filters in order to show the real, because it considers livestream selling still belongs to e-commerce. That is why none of its livestream hosts are on the blacklist, which the China Association of Performing Arts issued for prohibiting live broadcast. Taobao livestreaming platform has its view on the industry standard, which believes live e-commerce now is still at an early stage and thus, measures must be made to promote its growth in the future. It holds that livestream selling does not belong to advertisements which demand endorsement fees, and the livestream host is not the spokesperson of the ad and they just recommend the product. It suggests that the classification of livestream hosts should not be uniform and an inclusive and prudent attitude should be adopted. Since 2016, Taobao livestreaming platform has accumulated a large amount of experience on livestream hosts to access and business management. It is also ready to formulate industry standards with its peers to promote the sustainable and healthy development of the industry.

(2) ByteDance—Tik Tok livestreaming platform

As a short video live broadcast platform, Tik Tok's e-commerce links can access Taobao platform, JD.COM platform, Kuaishou. The platform pushes personalized content, with about 600 million active users per day in terms of traffic, and the age of users is mainly between 30 and 40. For Tik Tok, it still concentrates on creating a platform for the user to record their life, and livestream selling is not at its core strategy in the future. Currently, livestream hosts in Tik Tok who publish ten short videos with more than 1000 fans can sell goods.

Traditional e-commerce is based on graphic search, while Tik Tok uses influencer and KOL marketing based on discovery. It is worth mentioning that the sales volume of jade has quadrupled since it was sold through livestreaming. In Tik Tok, the head influencers have not occupied a large amount of traffic, and the distribution was relatively uniform on the whole. Tik Tok helped traditional folk artists to sell handicrafts such as oil-paper umbrellas, one of the national intangible cultural heritage, creating great industry benefits and social benefits.

---

[1] Data Source: collected by Government website.

Table 4.1 Live e-commerce industry support policies in some regions

Publishing unit	Policy document	Release date	Content
Guangzhou Municipal Bureau of Commerce	Guangzhou Live E-commerce Development Action Plan (2020–2022)	2020.03	Make Guangzhou a live e-commerce city
Shanghai	Shanghai Action Plan for Promoting Online New Economy Development (2020–2022)	2020.03	Promote the intelligent development of live e-commerce and social e-commerce new formats
Sichuan province	New Highland Action Plan for Live E-commerce Network Traffic of Quality Sichuan Goods (2020–2022)	2020.04	Pay close attention to 1000 ecological enterprises. After two years, the turnover of live broadcast goods reached 10 billion yuan and the output value exceeded 100 billion yuan.
Qingdao city	Qingdao Live E-commerce Development Action Plan (2020–2022)	2020.05	Form a live e-commerce industry cluster, support the formation of demonstrations by head anchor institutions, encourage the cultivation of MCN institutions, and create a certain number of online celebrity brands and KOLs
Chongqing	Chongqing Municipality Accelerates the Development of Live Broadcasting Action Plan	2020.05	Take the live broadcast and the online celebrity economy as a new driving force to promote economic development
Jinan city	Vigorously develop e-commerce economy and build the implementation plan of live stream economy headquarters base	2020.05	Make Jinan a well-known live stream economy headquarters in China
Guangzhou city	Measures for Supporting the Development of E-commerce Live Broadcasting in Huadu District of Guangzhou City (2020–2022)	2020.06	Establish ten live e-commerce bases, attract 100 live demonstration shops, and train 1000 live broadcast e-commerce retail sales exceeding 100 billion
Hangzhou city	12 live e-commerce support policies	2020.06	Create a complete live broadcast ecosystem

(continued)

Table 4.1 (continued)

Publishing unit	Policy document	Release date	Content
Yiwu, Zhejiang	Action Plan for Accelerating the Development of Live E-commerce in Yiwu City	2020.06	Create a first-class product supply chain system in online celebrity, promote the ecological perfection of live broadcast e-commerce, and foster new economic growth points

After the two sessions, the government has tightened supervision, putting much pressure on enterprises. Currently, false propaganda, fake sales, link problems and offline transactions out of management in the livestreaming industry have brought many difficulties to supervision and changed its model. The traditional way of oversight is to browse pictures and texts, while the videos of livestreaming selling has created troubles to supervision. Some livestream hosts have abandoned the oral presentation, using code words and photos to generate traffic, which needs more rules to regulate in the future. Government should take enterprises' suggestions into consideration. It is also feasible to entrust supervision to the platform, and the data should be obtainable. For example, different departments should set a standard for the validity of the product certificate, and avoid overlapping supervision. As the standards vary from departments and regions, it is necessary to coordinate all parties to observe actively. With the short video platform being popular, we need to formulate monitoring rules according to the actual business. That is how we maintain the competition rules, and keep competition fair and beneficial.

As for the difference between livestream e-commerce and traditional e-commerce, there are not too many law violations in livestream selling. With the number of fake ads linked with credit grade, once the points are deducted, the livestream hosts will have no chance to appear at the platform. As for the false propaganda, the accountability system must be established to define individuals' responsibilities clearly.

(3) Kuaishou livestreaming platform

Kuaishou e-commerce is committed to helping ordinary people share their lives, focusing on the interaction of netizens. In 2018, it launched projects of livestream commerce and short video plus e-commerce. The first e-commerce live broadcast in Kuaishou came from user "猫控小明君," who tested products for two hours and got busy selling goods all night long. In 2020, it participated in the fighting against the COVID-19 epidemic and resuming work and production. Going head, Kuaishou e-commerce will develop new businesses in domestic goods, rural commerce, public welfare, entertainment, crafts, education and so on. As for business models, livestream hosts conduct live broadcasts on short video and livestreaming platforms, with commodity links transferred to the CPS platform and then to the seller to complete the transaction. Kuaishou has built its own platform governance audit system, platform non-compliance punishment system and platform governance after-sales system. It formulated relevant rules from the platform perspective and has been committed to promoting industry self-discipline.

(4) JD.COM livestreaming platform

Established on September 11, 2016, the JD.COM livestreaming platform now handles 15,000 transactions per day. JD.COM has banned off-site transactions, with a complete closed-loop purchase from picking-up, all based on shopping. The positioning and value of live broadcast in JD.COM are a new channel of self-operation for merchants, a new scene of platform influence for platforms and a brand-new shopping experience for users. There are four main lines:

(i) Merchant livestream, which will be broadcasted on a large scale in the form of "President's Price Arrival," trump card alliance, Fushi curator, county magistrate live broadcast and platform generation broadcast.
(ii) Influencer livestream, ecological construction of talents in JD.COM institutions, the introduction of talents such as Wang Ziru and Wang Zijian, and Influence Challenge.
(iii) Pan-entertainment livestream, with JD.COM characteristic live broadcast content, live star broadcast, concert, music IE, entertainment IP, etc.
(iv) Livestream enabling, product and data infrastructure construction, and output of live broadcasting capability to various businesses. In the livestream of the newcomers, JD.COM gives many measures, including preferential flow, subsidies for screenings, doubling of commissions, etc. From industry perspective, false propaganda, grey industry chains are common to see, and users' rights are difficult to protect.

Chapter 5
Digital Security

Abstract In the era of digital economy, digital security, an elementary requirement, serves as a driving force for the development of industry and society. The crack on digital security not only threatens traditional sectors such as education and medical care, but also increases the risks in emerging technology fields such as artificial intelligence (AI), cloud computing, big data, the internet of things and blockchains. Now with China's digital economy booming, digital security problems continue to emerge. Chinese government has made great efforts in public data sharing, consumer personal data protection, and cross-border data flow, which build a digital security ecosystem to resist network security risks and create a firewall for the growth of the digital economy. When constructing the digital security evaluation index system of the digital business environment, we consider two aspects of network security and data security, and establish two primary indicators and six secondary indicators, in which the primary indicators are network security and data security, and three secondary indicators are set up to measure them concretely.

5.1 New Risks of Digital Security and Its Technical Protection Measures

With the rapid development of the digital economy, the collecting and use of information are becoming increasingly common. A large amount of data has also fallen into the new targets of cyber attackers and criminals. For example, in 2018, the system of a health company in Singapore has suffered from hacking, with 1.5 million people's personal information stolen, including the patient's name, nationality, address, gender, race and date of birth. The total population of Singapore is just about 6 million, which means one in four people in Singapore has his information leaked. In fact, since 2018, the incidence of cyber-attacks on traditional industries and critical social infrastructure such as government agencies has been at a high level. A large number of cyber-attacks and ransomware viruses have broken out and spread at home and abroad, taking a terrible toll on public infrastructures including governments, universities and hospitals, with multiple files and applications being

X. Li et al., *Development Practice of Digital Business Environment in China*, Applied Economics and Policy Studies,
https://doi.org/10.1007/978-981-16-8527-9_5

manipulated or damaged, which seriously hindered the operation of these institutions. It is an indisputable fact that cybersecurity has become a universal issue, and cyber-attacks are posing an unprecedented threat to all kinds of industries and each aspect of social activity.

Network security and data security are two important aspects of digital security at present. The so-called digital security means that in the computer network environment, the information is not tampered. The network is not damaged, and the computer hardware and software are not damaged. From a technical point of view, the definition of digital security can be understood. By adopting various technologies and management measures, the network system can run normally, thus ensuring the availability, integrity and confidentiality of network data.

5.1.1 New Risks of Digital Security in the Digital Economy Era

In the whole process of information development, from the host age to the network age, from the Internet age to the intelligent age, the concept of digital security has also experienced the development from 1.0 to 2.0, even 3.0. In the past, the public and even companies only stayed at the level of 1.0 for Internet information security. At this stage, individuals and enterprises only need to protect themselves, while enterprises need to protect their internal data, while individuals stay at the level of installing antivirus software to protect personal computer security. At this time, network information security is still very basic. However, this understanding is outdated under the tide of "internet plus", and network information security must evolve and upgrade with the deepening of "internet plus". In the "internet plus", a series of things such as the Internet of Everything, cloud computing, big data, smart home, smart travel, etc. are all inseparable from the support of network data. After all enterprises, families and individuals' devices are networked, the whole industry needs to cooperate, and security will permeate every link in the industrial chain.

In this era, instead of relying on a PC software to realize the protection stage of information security 1.0 and network security 2.0, it should belong to the brand-new digital security 3.0 stage-security integration and any link in the industrial chain. At this stage, digital security exposes many new risks:

First, there is a high incidence of data leakage. At present, data leakage presents the characteristics of increasingly intensified situation, increasingly diversified subjects, increasingly wide scope and increasingly complex industries. According to the data of network security company RBS, in the first three quarters of 2019, there were 5183 global data leakage incidents, an increase of 33% year-on-year. Second, the phenomenon of illegal collection of personal information is frequent. At present, the problems of compulsory authorization, excessive claim of rights and over-limit collection are still outstanding. In 2019, the Central Network Information Office and the four ministries and commissions jointly launched the special governance of

App's illegal collection and use of personal information, and received more than 12,000 pieces of reported information and verified more than 2300 problematic APPs throughout the year. Third, the situation of illegal data transactions intensified. According to the data of the National Internet Emergency Center, in 2019, the number of violent attacks against databases exceeded 10 billion times per day, and the dark network has become an important place for illegal data transactions.

In 2020, COVID-19 epidemic raged all over the world, catalyzing various industries to accelerate digital transformation, and the value of data was further highlighted, and data leakage continued to occur frequently. As shown in Tables 5.1 and 5.2, data leakage incidents occurred frequently in China and around the world, resulting in great losses to enterprises' assets and reputation. The public was deeply troubled by privacy exposure and harassment fraud.

Behind these real and vivid cases, the public was forced to suffer from privacy exposure, harassment and fraud, the loss of business data assets and the collapse of brand reputation, and some more serious data leaks, even threatening social stability and national security. It is urgent to prevent data leakage and protect data security.

Second, the content security risks are more prominent. The development of the Internet broadens people's information acceptance, and a large amount of information is exposed in public cyberspace, including a large amount of information with digital security risks. Specifically, the content security risks in digital security are mainly manifested in: (1) Political security issues. According to the research team of new york University, through the review of Facebook advertising database from May 2018 to June 2019, it was found that there were 86,000 pages with misleading political advertisements, about 37 million US dollars. (2) Dissemination of harmful information. In recent years, criminals have illegally produced, stored, disseminated

Table 5.1 Inventory of some data leakage events in China in 2020

Date	Events
January 20	Over 200 million pieces of user information of China Telecom were sold
March 19	Weibo's 538 million user data is sold on the dark network
April 16	The list of more than 6000 people in Jiaozhou Central Hospital in Qingdao, China was leaked
April 27	Hundreds of G video materials of bilibili's well-known UP master "Dang Mei" were stolen
May 6	CITIC Bank illegally divulges the personal privacy of talk show artists
May 20	Construction Bank employees sell more than 50,000 pieces of customer information
July 1	A decoration company in Sichuan, China spent 2.4 million to buy owner information
August 13	More than 6000 zhenai account information was stolen
September 7	Yuantong "inner ghost" leaked 400,000 customer information
October 15	Taizhou police cracked a case of infringing citizens' personal information, involving more than 8 million pieces of data

Table 5.2 Global inventory of some data leakage events in 2020

Date	Events
February 11	The data of 6.4 million voters in Israel was leaked
February 21	MGM hotel data dump 10.6 million passenger information leaked
March 23	British security company Cloud leaked 5 billion security records
April 11	Magellan's health was attacked by ransomware and data leaked
April 23	267 million Facebook account information is sold on the dark network
May 8	Indonesian e-commerce giant Tokopedia 9000 million account information is sold on the dark network
May 26	Thai mobile operator AIS Cloud leaked 8.3 billion Internet records
June 8	The WordPress database of millions of websites was stolen
June 22	Oracle leaked billions of network data records
July 25	Nintendo leaked a lot of internal games and equipment information
August 8	Ter 20GB internal data leakage
August 20	American AI company was exposed to leak nearly 2.6 million medical data
September 10	SK Hynix and LG Electronics leaked a lot of confidential information
September 21	FinCEN confidential documents leaked from the US Financial Crime Enforcement Network Bureau
October 15	Barnes&Noble, an online bookstore, was hacked, and consumers' mailboxes and purchase records were leaked
November 4	Swedish insurance giant Folksam data leak
November 10	Spanish Prestige software leaked the personal data of hotel guests
December 4	Brazil's Ministry of Health has serious loopholes in official website, and 243 million Brazilians' personal information has been leaked
December 8	Italian defense giant Leonardo S.p.A10GB confidential data leaked
December 16	Online exposure of 45 million medical images worldwide

and sold harmful information such as pornography, violence and terror by means of niche, encryption and cloud. (3) False news propaganda. According to the disclosure of the British government, more than 70 false news cases were detected every week during the epidemic.

Third, infrastructure security risks spill over. With the application of information systems and various intelligent devices in all walks of life, the key network infrastructure will become the battlefield in the future. All cyber warfare attacks are not only aimed at stealing intelligence as in the past, but can now launch attacks on infrastructure such as transportation, energy and finance, which can achieve better destructive effects than traditional operations. For example, in 2019, attacks against power systems occurred frequently all over the world, and the resulting power outages had a serious impact on society. In addition, according to the data of China National Internet Emergency Center, in 2019, DDoS attacks on Chinese cloud platforms accounted for 74% of attacks on domestic targets. The number of overseas attacks on large-scale industrial Internet cloud platforms reached 90 times a day, up 43% year-on-year. It has been attacked by more than 30 APT organizations throughout the year, and has expanded into many fields such as energy and finance.

5.1.2 *Technical Means of Digital Security Protection*

In the whole process of our development, we basically take host security as the core in the host era, and in the network era, we are characterized by information security 1.0. The characteristics of 2.0 are just need + compliance, and the characteristics of 3.0 have entered a very typical characteristic of aggregation ecology and key prevention and control of data security risks. Specifically, the current digital security mainly includes network security and data security.

(1) Network security

Cyber Security means that the hardware and software of the network system and the data in the system are protected from being damaged, changed or leaked due to accidental or malicious reasons. The system runs continuously, reliably and normally, and the network service is uninterrupted. Network security mainly includes information level security and operation level security, in which information level security mainly includes the production, storage, dissemination and sale of information such as false news, political rumors, distorted propaganda and pornography, while operation level mainly focuses on network attacks, network stealing, security loopholes and malicious programs.

As we all know, there is no absolute security in this world. We usually reduce network threats through security equipment and technology, security system, emergency response mechanism and so on. At present, the commonly used network security protection technologies mainly include firewall technology, anti-virus software, encryption technology, intrusion detection technology, etc., as shown in Table 5.3.

(2) Data security

With the continuous progress of information technology, massive amounts of data are coming, and human beings are striding into the era of big data. This big data, comparable to oil and gold, has become an important social wealth and a national

Table 5.3 Common technical means of network security protection

Technical name	Explanation
Firewall technology	It is mainly achieved by controlling network access rights
Antivirus software	Effectively monitor and kill malware, Trojan viruses and computer viruses
Encryption technology	Scrambling the original file information in the computer
Intrusion detection	Complement the protection wall technology to realize early warning and hinder intrusion

basic strategic resource. A large number of semi-structured and unstructured data have emerged and become mainstream, and their complexity makes the threats and challenges faced by data security grow nonlinearly with the scale of data.

The problem of data security includes two levels: First, the information security of social subjects, such as individual citizens or business subjects. In fact, in the era of big data information, everyone is transparent. To protect privacy and security, it is necessary to restrict access to personal information. However, for ordinary people, information security is relatively weak. For example, when using some tools and software such as APP, there are many mandatory overlord clauses. Only by choosing consent can we proceed to the next step, and choosing consent, personal information is bound to be. Therefore, in order to protect people's privacy, it is necessary for the state to issue regulations, such as collecting only information necessary for business. In addition, public information can only be used for product optimization and cannot be used for profit; If personal information is sold as a commodity, it will violate the privacy of social subjects. Whether it is an enterprise or an individual, privacy and security will be seriously leaked. This point must be refined and regulated by laws and regulations. The second level involves national security. For example, government information and enterprise information should not and are not allowed to be transferred abroad. At this point, the United States has requirements for Chinese enterprises, and China should also have requirements for foreign enterprises. Data collected in China can only be stored in China. From the perspective of national security, the information of Chinese enterprises cannot be collected by foreign enterprises or institutions at will, which is an urgent security issue.

In this context, the need to protect personal privacy and ensure data integrity, confidentiality and availability is highlighted by means of data encryption, data desensitization, data leakage prevention, data tracing and database security. At the same time, major countries in the world are also actively researching and breaking through core technologies and exploring the construction of data security technology solutions. Specifically, the current development trend of data security technology mainly includes the following aspects:

(1) Sensitive data identification technology is developing towards intelligence.

First, on the basis of traditional keyword recognition, related enterprises expand the recognition scope and improve the recognition accuracy by introducing rules matching, natural language processing and other technologies. Second, combined with cluster analysis and other machine learning technologies, the intelligent degree of sensitive data identification is improved through the cumulative training of big data.

(2) Data tracking and tracking technology is in the research and development stage.

First, digital watermarking technology, whose technical realization principle is to embed data watermark into data content through information processing without affecting data reading and application, so as to realize data marking and tracking. At present, because of its high occupation and high dependence on processing resources and storage resources, digital watermarking technology is mostly suitable for relatively stable small data sets, and cannot be applied to cloud computing, big data and other large-scale data aggregation scenarios. The second is data blood tracing technology. The main technical principle is to record the data flow process in real time, trace and analyze the causes of data security incidents, and reduce security risks.

(3) Data encryption technology is developed in different scenarios.

One is reversible encryption, in which data is encrypted by a specific algorithm and then becomes cipher text. Only through the corresponding key can cipher text be decrypted into plaintext. Reversible encryption technology is used for digital certificates and daily file encryption in online payment. The other is irreversible encryption. The data processed by irreversible encryption algorithm can't recover plaintext, so the same data can only be encrypted again by using the same algorithm, and verified by comparing cipher text.

(4) The research and application of data anonymity technology is accelerated.

Anonymization technology refers to transforming data according to a specific algorithm, ensuring that data cannot be located to individuals and cannot be restored while ensuring the availability of data, so as to achieve the purpose of protecting individual privacy information. At present, anonymous technologies mainly include differential privacy, anonymity and so on. In recent years, data anonymity technology has been widely concerned by the industry and applied in data exchange and data analysis. For example, in the international arena, Apple has applied differential privacy technology in search prediction. Domestically, Alibaba's data anonymity technology has also made great progress.

5.2 Status of Creating Digital Security Environment

In the era of the digital economy, digital security, which represents an elementary ability, serves as a driving force for the development of industry and society. The loopholes in digital security not only threaten traditional sectors such as education and medical care, but also increase the risks in emerging technology fields such as artificial intelligence (AI), cloud computing, big data, the internet of things and blockchains. Now with China's digital economy booming, digital security problems continue to emerge. The Chinese government has made great efforts in public data sharing, consumer personal data protection, and cross-border data flow, which build a digital security ecosystem to resist network security risks and create a firewall for the growth of the digital economy.

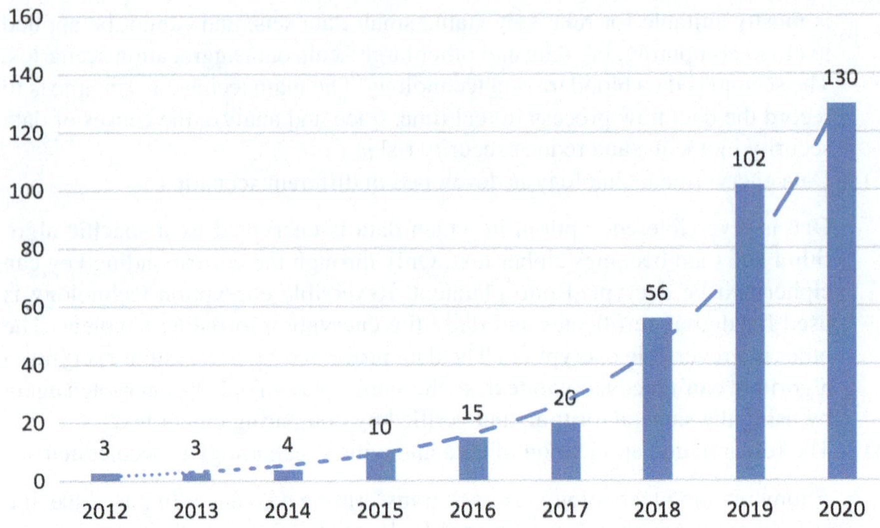

Fig. 5.1 Growth in the number of open platforms for local government data in China over the past year

5.2.1 Government Public Data Open and Sharing

Opening government public data means that the government will open its data that does not involve state secrets, national security, and personal privacy to the public under the law and regulations, with particular emphasis on the original data. This is different from the traditional sense of government information disclosure. Government information disclosure means that the original data are made public after a conclusion is reached by integrating specific resources. Currently, the Chinese government has a considerable amount of public data resources that can be opened and shared, covering macro-economy, land resources, urban and rural construction, public transportation, social security, public safety, medical and health care, education, and culture and other fields. As shown in Figs. 5.1, 5.2. As of the end of April 2020, 17 provincial governments, 113 sub-provincial and prefecture-level governments in China have launched data open platforms; 54.83% of the provincial administrative regions (Hong Kong, Macao and Taiwan are omitted), 73.33% of the sub-provincial and 32.08% of the prefecture-level administrative areas have launched government data open platforms.[1]

At the data level, most of the current data open platforms can provide data of great varieties, wide range and high quality according to its administrative levels. For example, the Tianjin Information Resources Unified Open Platform currently has open data, covering 21 topics, from 51 municipal departments, 16 districts, with

[1] Data Source: 2020 Chinese Local Government Data Open Report.

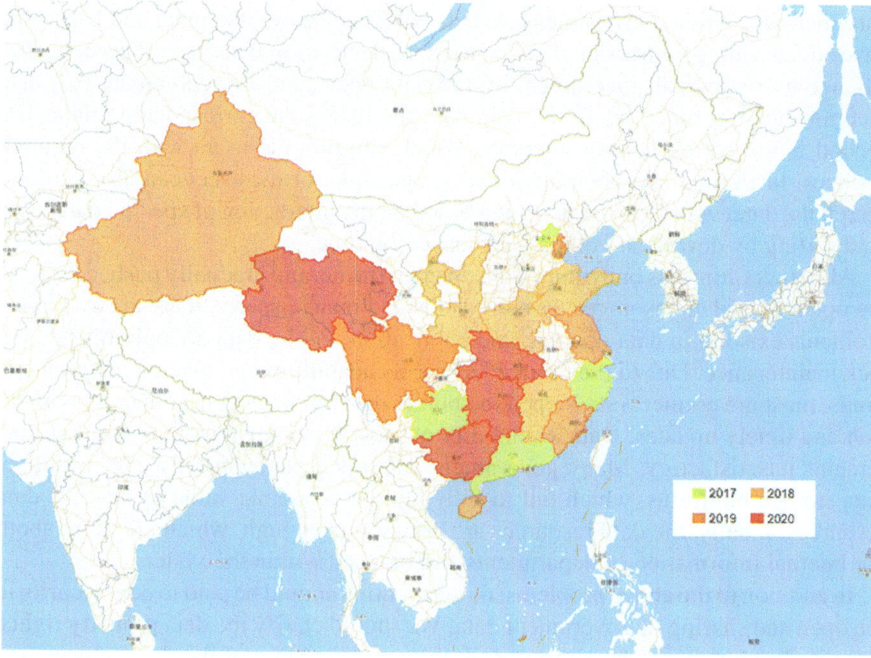

Fig. 5.2 Geographical spatial distribution of online time of data open platforms (provincial level)

1033 data sets and 562 data interfaces.[2] Fujian Public Information Resources Open Platform has opened 623.762 pieces of million data, and 702 sets of resources, with 1427 APIs and 39 departments.[3] The Guangzhou municipal government data unified open platform has opened 63 departments and 1522 data sets, with 1,376,635 available data and 171,868 downloads.[4] Meanwhile, each platform also provides a variety of data formats, such as XLS, ZIP, XLM, DOC, CSV, JSON, etc., to meet different download requirements.

In terms of data organization and retrieval, studies will be carried from the perspective of classification. The vast majority of municipal government websites can be divided into two modes according to their content or source, making the operation more effortless. Based on this, Shanghai city government has improved its website classification. In contrast, Zhengzhou city government has added various labels, which can help users quickly find different subjects and data providers, thus reducing the complexity in the process of data information retrieval. After classifying data resources, in order to further improve the convenience of data retrieval, data open websites provide a variety of retrieval functions. Most of the government data open platforms offer website retrieval functions, including keyword retrieval and

[2] Data Source: https://data.tj.gov.cn/.

[3] Data Source: https://data.fujian.gov.cn/odweb/.

[4] Data Source: https://data.gz.gov.cn/.

classified navigation. Government websites of Zhengzhou, Shanghai and Changsha have added a large number of cross-restricted selections in the retrieval process. The Chongqing municipal government affairs data open platform can create two data recommendation functions for all data sets: the first is the corresponding data. The second is the corresponding interface, which can provide users with the required services. In Beijing and Nanjing administration platforms, users can also sort and search the data, which can be designed based on the interaction of specific data, with data sorting by download volume and sorting by time.

Although China has built many data open platforms and gradually pushed forward the opening of data resources in many fields and many aspects, there are still many problems existing in data opening and application. Public data are only opened but lack maintenance. Due to the limited technical capabilities and insufficient financial funds, most governments only open the public data but neglect necessary classification and timely updates. Data availability of most government data open platforms remains unsatisfactory. Many government data open platform only acts as simple data storage platforms, which fail to fully tap the economic value of massive data resources. Finally, the data resources are not mobile enough, which are more about the internal information of departments and blocked within the system.

In addition to the above problems, more attention should be paid to data security in the open and sharing of government data. We should clarify the data property rights, draw a clear line between the responsibilities and freedom of the data subject, and distinguish what data can be opened and what data cannot be opened, conditional or unconditional. Opening state-secret data to researchers properly can help them carry out innovative research and thus promote social progress. At the same time, we need to control confidential data, safeguarding national security. Therefore, whether to open the data and how much to be opened should be decided carefully. Public data is taken from the people and used for the people. To make public data serve the people in a better and safer way, the significant issues have been on the top agenda of the governments.

5.2.2 Consumer Personal Data Protection

In the epoch of digital economy, artificial intelligence, big data, internet business, blockchain, internet of things, and social media are closely related to the generation of personal data, and private information collection has become commonplace. In daily life, information is collected according to policies and regulations or because of trade in medical, transportation, accommodation, banking, insurance, real estate, logistics and other industries. However, now even private service fields such as catering, retail and even fitness institutions are keen to collect people's personal information. More and more personal information is obtained by institutions and entities, so there is no basic guarantee for information security. With privacy data leaked now and then, personal privacy is not guaranteed.

Personal data is also referred to as personal information in some legal documents. The definition of personal data in the General Data Protection Regulations is any information related to "identified or identifiable" natural persons (data subjects). In the United States, the definition of personal data is more specific in the California Consumer Privacy Act, which considers that personal information refers to information that can be identified, correlated, described, and associated or reasonably associated with a particular consumer or family, but does not contain publicly available information, de-identified or aggregated consumer information.

The protection of personal data was initially carried out within the framework of the right to privacy. European Union has been exploring the rules protecting personal data from the European Convention on Human Rights. Later the concept of "right to personal data protection" was put forward in the Charter of Fundamental Rights of the European Union. General Data Protection Regulation clearly defines the right to personal data protection. With the popularity of the Internet and the development of the digital economy, the connotation and extension of privacy have gradually expanded, including not only sensitive and private information but also all kinds of information that can identify personal attributes and behavioral characteristics. Based on the advancement of the new-generation digital information technology applications such as machine learning, deep learning, reinforcement learning, and neural networks, fragmented and one-sided information that initially does not involve citizens' sensitive and private information can be integrated and mined in a short time, and then accurate analysis reports can be obtained. The traditional protection based on personality and privacy can no longer meet the needs of people and the demands of society. Laws should give clear definitions and special protection to personal data in addition to the right to privacy.

As the economic value of personal data is exploited, confidential data leakage and abuse have become increasingly severe. One of the main ways of confidential data leakage is for operators to collect personal data without their consent. The other is for operators or criminals to intentionally disclose, sell or illegally provide personal data to others, including the leakage of personal information caused by loopholes in the network service system, theft by criminals through Trojans, phishing websites, defrauding personal information and operators' collecting unnecessary personal data. Personal data leakage takes various forms and brings other harms, which are mainly manifested as exposure of behavior records, harassment by spam and phone calls, personal property damage due to fraud, and even threats to the life safety of citizens.

For a long time, although China has continuously issued legislative documents on personal information protection, there has never been a system of laws and regulations and comprehensive legislation on issues related to personal information protection. Judging from the existing laws, including Civil Code, Criminal Law, Electronic Commerce Law, Cyber Security Law, Consumer Rights Protection Law and Advertising Law, although some contents are consistent with the topic of personal information protection, in social practice, the application of these laws mostly stipulates relatively principles, which cannot meet the urgent needs of the people for personal information protection. In addition, looking at other regulations and normative documents, such as "Decision on Strengthening Network Information Protection", "Regulations on the Protection of Personal Information of Telecommunications and Internet Users", "Specifications for Personal Information Security of Information Security Technology" (GB/T 35273-2020), etc., although they play a very strong reference value in the case handling of lawyers, they also have a certain lag, which cannot meet the compliance needs of various Internet enterprises. Under the background that China's personal information protection legislation is not perfect for a long time, in recent years, cases of personal information abuse have emerged constantly, which has brought great challenges to judicial and administrative supervision departments. Finally, on October 21, 2020, the Law Commission of the Standing Committee of Chinese Adults released the draft of the Personal Information Protection Law of the People's Republic of China (hereinafter referred to as "Personal Information Protection Law"), and publicly solicited opinions on the legislative issues related to personal information protection. This Personal Information Protection Law is about to be pushed to the historical stage, waiting for its brilliant chapter.

In addition to legislation to protect consumers' personal data, the government, enterprises and individuals also create a personal data security environment through various technical and management means, such as using cryptographic technology to encrypt storage and transmission of personal data, and using isolation and access control technology to implement strict access control of personal data. Taking LBS (location-based service) as an example, these service systems often collect users' location data without users' knowledge, and analyze and process these data. Therefore, how to protect the user's location privacy has become an urgent problem to be solved. The commonly used LBS privacy protection technologies are shown in Table 5.4.

At present, China has defined the nature of the data through legislation, explained the property attributes of the data, made a general stipulation that the personal data of natural persons are protected by law, and defined the legal consequences of illegal collection, acquisition and use of personal data. The government, enterprises and individuals have also created a secure environment for personal data through various means from the technical and management aspects, such as using cryptographic technology to implement encrypted storage and transmission of personal data, and using isolation and access control technology to take strict access control of personal data. However, incidents of personal data leakage are still occurring one after another. Therefore, how to protect personal data in the current rapid development of the digital economy is undoubtedly an intricate problem that the government, enterprises and individuals have to face.

Table 5.4 Common LBS privacy protection technologies

Type of technology	Problem scenario	Common technical means
Technology based on distortion	Position data	Pseudonym[a], randomization[b], concealment[c]
	Trajectory data	Dynamic pseudonym, false track[d]
Encryption-based technology	Position/trajectory data	PIR[e], Spatial transformation[f]
Differential privacy technology	Trajectory data	CDP[g]
	Position data	LDP[h]

[a]The idea of pseudonym replacement method is that when a user sends a query request, the user's real name can be deleted and replaced by a temporary name, which is only an identifier and does not contain the user's identity information

[b]Randomization uses distributed architecture, which means that in LBS query, in order to protect users' real location information and query content, dummy is randomly added, and dummy query is sent to LSP together with users' real query

[c]Concealment uses distributed structure, which refers to deleting or hiding LBS query information of users in LSP

[d]Its basic idea is to build multiple false trajectories for users' real trajectories to reduce the risk of privacy leakage

[e]Distributed architecture is adopted, which does not need TTP and does not rely on third-party intermediate processing

[f]Using encryption technology, the location information and POI information in LBS query are converted to Hilbert value in one-dimensional encryption space, and the query is evaluated in this space, so that there is still a certain correspondence between the converted data and the original data

[g]Centralized differential privacy, based on centralized architecture, the original data is centrally managed by a third-party server, and the data query and release based on differential privacy protection technology are uniformly provided to the outside world

[h]Localized differential privacy local differential privacy is based on distributed architecture. Users can handle sensitive data privately locally, which protects private data from the root cause and avoids privacy leakage caused by the intervention of third-party servers

5.2.3 Cross-Border Data Flow

The concept of cross-border data flow can be traced back as early as 1980 when The Organization for Economic Development and Cooperation (OECD) defined individuals' cross-border data flow as "the movement of personal data across national boundaries" in OECD Guidelines on the Protection of Privacy and Transborder Flows of Personal Data. At present, there is no consensus for the definition of cross-border data flow among international organizations, but it can be classified into two categories by whether or not they cross national borders: one is the transmission, processing and storage of data across national borders; the other is that data can be accessed by third-country entities even though they do not yet cross the national borders. As a new factor of production, data flowing between different industries has created tremendous value, with its contribution to global economic growth even exceeding the traditional elements represented by goods, services, capital and trade. From 2009 to 2018, the gift of global cross-border data flow to global economic growth reached 10.1%.[5]

The cross-border flow of data creates value for the enterprise and stakeholders, but on the other hand, generates a series of risks. From the perspective of enterprises, the risk brought by the cross-border flow of data is essentially a data security problem, which is caused by data leakage or abuse during or after the movement. However, from the perspective of countries, the risk is not only concerning the enterprise itself, but also correlates the national data security and public data security during or after the flow, which brings new business risks to the enterprise.

In the era of data economy, the data security risks in the cross-border flow involve legislative, political and economic aspects, which includes:

(1) Disclosure of personal data privacy.

Personal data is the central part of the cross-border data flow, but personal data protection varies from countries and regions. The flow of personal data from countries/regions with higher protection levels to countries/areas with lower protection levels will increase the risk of personal data privacy leakage.

(2) Foreign government data monitoring.

The cross-border data flow involves the export of domestic data to other countries, so the chances are that important or sensitive data is leaked and used. Because data resources (including personal data) may involve national intelligence, it inevitably risks disclosing state secrets in cross-border flow activities.

(3) Difficulties in enforcement by the government.

The cross-border data flow makes it more difficult for governments to obtain corporate data, which increases the uncertainty of law enforcement. The data of an enterprise may be stored in the "cloud" of another country, while an enterprise that provides digital infrastructure can also serve enterprises in multiple countries at the same time. Global interdependence makes it more challenging to establish substantive national security review and normalized security supervision over the primary network and even causes management conflicts in different countries.

Although there are many risks in cross-border data flow, as a new labor factor, it can bring considerable economic value to countries all over the world. However, in recent years, there are still major differences between countries on whether the data cross-border is based on the principle of free flow and whether the data cross-border control is justified. China's Data Security Law (Draft) puts forward the data security free flow principle for the first time, taking data free flow as the basic principle and data security flow as the restrictive principle, so as to balance the dual goals

[5] Zhang Monan. Cross-border Data Flow Being a New Focus of Games Between Major Powers [J/OL]. Finance and Economy, 2021(02):1 [2021-03-07]. http://kns.cnki.net/kcms/detail/36.1005.F.20210225.1113.013.html.

of opening up to the outside world and national security, and provide a prudent, inclusive and cooperative Chinese plan for global data governance.

(1) Safe and free data exit system.

China's Guidelines for Data Outbound Security Assessment (Draft) focuses on the security protection capabilities and measures taken by the data sender and the data receiver to ensure the integrity, confidentiality and availability of the data and ensure the data outbound. At the same time, considering the variety of data types and values, we should follow the principle of data classification and make different situation rules for "important data" and "non-important data". Important data has always been the focus of China's data exit control. Article 28 of the Data Security Management Measures (Draft for Comment) stipulates that before providing important data to overseas, network operators should assess the possible security risks and report them to the competent regulatory authorities of the industry for approval. If the competent supervision department of the industry is not clear, it shall be approved by the provincial network information department.

(2) Safe and free data retrieval system.

All along, China's attitude towards overseas data retrieval has always adhered to the principle of free flow and avoided using unilateral power. However, with the globalization of Chinese enterprises, China's legislation in the data field is also facing "easy to attack and defend", and it is imperative to appropriately expand extraterritorial jurisdiction. In fact, under the background of internationalization and virtualization of crime, the cross-border collection of electronic evidence of Chinese unilateralism has become the norm. In 2016, "Provisions on Several Issues Concerning the Collection, Extraction, Examination and Judgment of Electronic Data in Criminal Cases" clarified the power of investigation organs to collect overseas data directly. Article 2 of the Data Security Law (Draft) continues and innovates the extraterritorial protective jurisdiction of Article 75 of the Cyber Security Law, which not only expands the protection of rights and interests, but also lowers the trigger threshold. Chinese law enforcement agencies should have the right to obtain overseas electronic evidence. At the same time, based on defensive data sovereignty, China has always restricted or prohibited data access from other countries. Article 33 of the Data Security Law (Draft) and Article 4 of the International Criminal Judicial Assistance Law are regarded as blocking decrees to deal with foreign long-arm jurisdiction.

5.3 Doing-Digital-Business Environment–Research on Digital Security Assessment Indicators

Digital security, an essential guarantee for the steady development of the digital economy, is a vital part in the optimization of the doing-digital-business environment, which makes digital security assessment an indispensable aspect in the evaluation in the department. Generally speaking, digital security is not only the base layer of network security in the traditional sense, but also includes the application layer of government public data open and sharing, consumers' data protection, cross-border data flow, etc. As the underlying part of digital security, network security refers to the technical means to ensure the safety of data sharing, personal data protection and cross-border data flow. The operating mechanism and regulation system are also included. Therefore, the digital security assessment should involve indicators of both the base layer and the application layer.

Based on this, when constructing the digital security evaluation index system of the digital business environment, we consider two aspects of network security and data security, and establish two first-level indicators and six second-level indicators, in which the first-level indicators are network security and data security, and three second-level indicators are set up under the two first-level indicators to measure them concretely.

(1) Network security indicators

The network security assessment in digital security should show the network condition in the investigated area and the costs that enterprises need to pay to further improve security compliance. Considering the availability, reliability and representativeness of data, the network security level 2 indicators are designed as follows: the construction of network security-related technology platforms, the occurrence of network security (including data security) events, the enterprises' network security condition and the costs that enterprises have to pay to meet network security compliance.

(i) The construction of network security related technology platform can reflect the importance attached to network security in the surveyed area. The investigation adopts a combination of qualitative and quantitative methods, and the specific problems can be designed as follows: Has the network security related technology platform and quantity been built in the region. If there is a network security Xiangguang technology platform, what is the scale of the platform? Visits? How often is the content updated?
(ii) Network security (including data security) incidents can reflect the reliability of network security in the area under investigation at present. This indicator uses quantitative methods to obtain relevant data, and the types of network security incidents are not limited to those shown in Table 5.5
(iii) "The situation of network security enterprises and the cost that enterprises need to pay to meet network security compliance", it can be directly obtained whether the digital business environment in the current surveyed area needs to start from the aspect of network security optimization.

(2) Data security indicators

Based on the analysis of the current situation of the digital security environment, the evaluation indicators of the application layer should design secondary indicators

Table 5.5 Common network security events

Type	Security event
Network attack	Denial of service attacks, backdoor attacks, vulnerability attacks, network scanning eavesdropping events, phishing events, interference events, etc.
Harmful program	Computer virus events, worm events, Trojan horse events, botnet events, mixed attacker events, malicious code embedded in web pages, and so on
Information disclosure	Patent disclosure, system active monitoring and abnormal bill checking, product bidding promotion, suspected employee leaking customer information, employee leaking company contract, etc.
Content security	Use the information network to publish and disseminate security incidents that endanger national security, social stability, public interests and company interests

from three aspects: the security of government public data sharing, the protection of consumer personal data, and the safety of cross-border data flow to measure the business convenience.

(i) The security of government public data open and sharing is measured by the construction of digital open platforms (types and number of data sets, number of API interfaces and downloads) and the favorable policies for data open and sharing. The construction of the data platform can reflect the current situation of the open sharing of government data in the surveyed areas. At present, special data open platforms have been set up in many places, and the online data of the platform can be easily queried on the platform, and the survey data is relatively easy to obtain. The policy support of data open sharing can reflect the attitude and support of the surveyed regional governments for public data open sharing, and the development trend of local government public data open sharing in the future can be inferred from this index.

(ii) The protection of consumer personal data is measured by the leakage of personal privacy data and the support policies of personal data privacy protection. The situation of personal privacy data leakage can reflect the protection intensity of personal privacy data in the investigated area. If there are many leakage incidents or leakage incidents with a bad degree, it means that the protection intensity of local consumers' privacy data is low and the protection benefit is not enough, otherwise it means that the protection intensity of personal privacy data in the investigated area is high. The support policy of personal privacy data protection can reflect the importance attached to personal privacy data protection in the surveyed areas. By analyzing the current privacy protection policies, we can also find out the current policy loopholes and guide the subsequent formulation of consumer privacy data protection policies.

(iii) The security of cross-border data flow is measured by the situation of unfavorable events of cross-border data flow and the rules of cross-border data flow (whether established or not and the degree of strict).

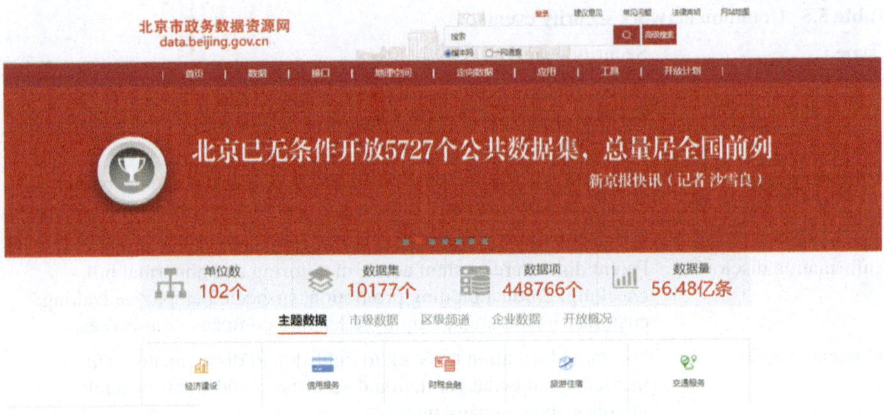

Fig. 5.3 Main station of Beijing Government Affairs data resource network

5.4 China's Digital Security Best Practices

5.4.1 Beijing Municipal Government Affairs Data Resources Network Promotes Public Data Sharing by Multi-means

The website was led by Beijing Economic and Information Technology Bureau, with the participation of all government departments in Beijing, and started trial operation in October 2012. This website is dedicated to providing download and service of all kinds of data that can be opened by Beijing government affairs department, providing data support for enterprises and individuals to develop and utilize government information resources in a socialized way, and promoting the development of information value-added service industry and related data analysis and research work.

Beijing municipal government affairs data resource network has built a "data opening and innovation base" and is the first to open medical insurance data in China. It has established a data service window to provide a new channel for data open consultation applications and set up a financial public data zone to give credit of 2 billion yuan to nearly 1000 small and micro-enterprises. By the end of 2020, Beijing has unconditionally opened 92 units, 5727 data sets and a total of about 5.76 million public data to the public through the government data resource network. With conditional access to data, the total number of open public data in Beijing has reached 9214 data sets and a total of 5.53 billion data records,[6] ranking first in China (Fig. 5.3).

Beijing Government Affairs Data Resource Network opened the Financial Public Data Zone for the first time, which lit up the blind zone of traditional financial inclusive services and made people see the efficacy of data opening. Up to now, Beijing Big Data Platform has been conditionally opened to the Financial Public Data

[6] Data Source: https://data.beijing.gov.cn/hdjl/ljhd/ggsjj/index.htm.

Zone, covering 3158 data items such as registration, tax payment, social security, real estate, patents and government procurement of more than 2 million market entities, with a total of more than 2.57 billion data records. It is reported that the special zone has provided strong support for the business handling of 27 financial institutions stationed in the first loan center, supporting it to provide registration financing needs for 14,913 enterprises, and approved 11,619 cases, involving an amount of about 42.5 billion yuan. Support the Inclusive Financing business of financial institutions, and push the credit line of 2 billion yuan for nearly 1000 small and micro enterprises in Beijing. We supported ICBC and China Construction Bank to launch Inclusive Financing products such as Inclusive Big Data Credit Loan and Yunyi Loan respectively, and granted loans totaling over RMB36 million to 28 SMEs.

There are more than 70 applications developed based on this website, such as Visit the Museum APP self-help tour, e-school, wisdom learning Road-Beijing road congestion analysis and prediction during students' commuting time, traffic map-urban traffic guidance information service system, SIG- intelligent government comprehensive service system, etc., as shown in Table 5.6.

Table 5.6 Related applications relying on the development of Beijing Government Affairs resource network (incomplete statistics)

Application name	Explain
Visit the museum	Voice navigation and indoor positioning software
E go to school	Intelligent screening matches the user's demand for admission to buy a house
Zhihuixue road	Analysis and Prediction of Beijing Road Congestion during Students' Commuting Time
A map of traffic	Urban traffic guidance information service system
Beijing tong APP	Mobile government affairs and public service platform
Beijing zhengxin	Export enterprise holographic portrait products
Baidu flying Paddle platform	Quickly get a special AI model suitable for your own scene
Xingyetong-Jianjie loan	Adopt credit guarantee-free method to provide self-service revolving loan quota
Loan and loan are safe	Provide a comprehensive financial service platform for small and micro customers
Oral safety	It is convenient and intuitive to know the registration information of food
Beside pets	"Nearby hospital", "tips for raising dogs", and "Taboo recipes" and other functions

5.4.2 Venustech Accentuates the Government's Support in Building Network Security

Founded in 1996, Venustech is the leading provider of network security products, trusted security management platforms, specialized security services and solutions. Venustech has dedicated itself to providing competitive proprietary products and best practice services, helping its customers fully promote the security capability and productive efficiency of their IT infrastructures. Trusted by its valued customers, the company has provided security equipment and solutions for over 30,000 users worldwide, including more than 30 firms of the fortune global 500, over 80% of Chinese banking institutions and over 60% of China's large state-owned enterprises, as well as all Chinese telecom carriers. Proud of its professional team, Venustech owns the first enterprise-level Postdoctoral Station for network security in the nation and the certified state-level network security R&D center with over 200 developers. Venustech has applied for hundreds of technical patents and won numerous pioneering achievements in the industry: China's first IDS hardware product, China's first distributed vulnerability scanning system, China's first 10 Gigabit multi-core UTM platform, and realization of a significant breakthrough in 10 Gigabit UTM core technology. To date, Venustech has discovered more than 1000 CVE vulnerabilities and exposures in total, holding the record across Asia. With its significant performance and achievements in the industry, Venustech was the first enterprise in China to join the Microsoft MAPP program.

5.4.3 TOPSEC Highlights Personal Data Protection

TOPSEC has led the development of network security technology, ranking first in China's network security firewall market for 20 consecutive years and leading the market in security hardware and overall network security. Over the years, TOPSEC has continued to innovate, taking the lead to launch the TOPSEC linkage agreement, "Trusted Network Architecture (TNA1.0)", "Trusted Network World (TNW)" and the "Next Generation Trusted Network Security Architecture (NGTNA)" with network security as the core, big data as the foundation and cloud services as the delivery model in China, and constructed a global security defense system with situational awareness and linkage protection.

In the mixed network world, TOPSEC believes that we should strictly control the illegal acts of violating personal privacy data and place personal data in a very vital place. At present, from seven aspects of users, applications, content, security, services, location and time, TOPSEC Credit is continuously building a solid network awareness system to safeguard personal data security from terminals, pipelines to the cloud, and is committed to comprehensively protecting user information and building a trusted network and a safe world for customers.

5.4.4 Many Provinces and Cities in China Have Issued Policies Related to Government Data Security

The Chinese government has fully emphasized the importance of digital security, especially data security, in the digital economy era. With the advancement of e-government, government affairs have gradually entered the electronic stage, resulting in a large number of government data, including many highly sensitive data, which will cause immeasurable losses once leaked or tampered. The protection of digital security needs to be considered from both institutional and technical aspects. As the regulatory body of social governance, the government mainly considers the protection mechanism of digital security from the aspects of institutional policies, laws and regulations. Based on this, governments around China have successively issued a number of laws and regulations related to digital security to regulate and punish acts endangering digital security. As shown in Table 5.7, it stipulates the basic principles that government data sharing should follow:

(1) Take sharing as the principle, with the exception of not sharing.

In principle, the government information resources formed by various government departments should be shared, and those involving state secrets and security should be implemented in accordance with relevant laws and regulations.

(2) Demand-oriented, free use.

Departments that need to use shared information due to their duties (hereinafter referred to as users) put forward clear sharing requirements and information use purposes, and departments that generate and provide shared information (hereinafter referred to as providers) should respond in time and provide shared services free of charge.

(3) Unified standards and overall construction.

Collect, store, exchange and share government information resources in accordance with the relevant standards of national government information resources, adhere to the principle of one number and one source, and make multiple checks, and make overall plans to build a catalogue system and share and exchange system of government information resources.

(4) Establish a mechanism to ensure safety.

The joint meeting will co-ordinate the establishment of a government information resource sharing management mechanism and an information sharing evaluation mechanism. All government departments and sharing platform management units should strengthen the identification, authorization management and security guarantee of the whole process of collecting, sharing and using shared information to ensure the security of shared information.

Table 5.7 Data security management regulations issued by Chinese municipal governments (incomplete statistics)

City Name	Name
Tianjin city	Tianjin Data Security Management Measures (Provisional)
Shijiazhuang city	Regulations of Shijiazhuang Municipality on Security Management of Government Data Resources Sharing
Cangzhou city	Measures for the Management of Big Data Resources in Cangzhou City
shenyang	Regulations of Shenyang Municipality on Sharing and Opening Government Data Resources
Nanjing	Interim Measures for the Administration of Government Affairs Data in Nanjing
Hangzhou city	Safety Management Specification for Government Data Sharing
Nanping City	Measures of Nanping Municipality on the Administration of Government Affairs Data
Ji'an	Interim Measures for the Management of Government Data Sharing in Ji'an City
Jining City	Measures for the Safety Management of Government Data in Jining City
Binzhou city	Interim Measures for the Administration of Binzhou Government Data Security
Liaocheng City	Interim Measures for the Management of Government Data Resources in Liaocheng City
Zhumadian city	Interim Measures for Security Management of Government Data in Zhumadian City
Changsha city	Notice of the Interim Measures for the Administration of Government Data Resources in Changsha City
Dongguan city	Administrative Measures of Dongguan Municipality on Sharing Government Data Resources (for Trial Implementation)
Tongren city	Detailed Rules for the Implementation of Government Data Security Management in tongren city
Xi'an	"Xi 'an government data resources sharing management measures"
Yanan City	Interim Measures for the Sharing and Management of Government Data Resources in Yan 'an City
Nanning city	Measures of Nanning Municipality on the Safety Management of Government Data
Qinzhou city	Qinzhou government data security management measures
Yulin city	Implementation Plan of Yulin Government Affairs Data Security

Chapter 6
Digital Services

Abstract The demands for the development of digital government services refer to the recognition and the promotion factors for it under the environment of digital economy. At present, the driving force for the development of China's digital government services generally comes from social demand and digital technology, etc. For the development of e-government in the digital age, social demand has been the basis. The technical support has been the driving force and medium. In the evaluation of digital government service level for China's digital business environment, we mainly inspected the level of digital government service platform, the development of government websites, the development of new government media and so on. It covered four measurable secondary indicators: the completeness of service mode, the coverage of service items, the accuracy of service guide and the maturity of online processing. And we gave two best practices of digital government services in China: Xiong'an new area, Hebei, China and Binhai New Area in Tianjin, China.

6.1 Demand of the Times for the Development of Digital Government Services

The demands of the times for the development of digital government services refer to the recognition of the development of digital government services or the promotion factors for the development of digital government services under the background of digital economy. At present, the driving force for the development of China's digital government services generally comes from social demand and digital technology, etc. For the development of e-government in the digital age, social demand is the basis and technical support is the driving force and medium.

6.1.1 Social Needs

The ultimate goal of developing digital government services is to enable the government to rationally allocate public resources to provide high-quality public goods and

X. Li et al., *Development Practice of Digital Business Environment in China*, Applied Economics and Policy Studies,
https://doi.org/10.1007/978-981-16-8527-9_6

services, so as to meet the diverse needs of the public. Therefore, the social demand for promoting the development of digital government services includes two aspects. One is the government demand, the other is the public demand.

(1) The government needs

Before the reform and opening up, China was under a strict planned economic system, which made China's public service supply system in the monopoly of the government for a long time. The government was the only producer and supplier of public services. This supply system brought great pressure to the government, but also brought many problems such as low quality of public service products. In this context, China's public service supply has opened a market-oriented reform path. Enterprises and non-profit organizations are introduced into the public service supply system as producers of public services, and the government is the party that buys services or outsources public services. By purchasing public services by the government, public service resources can be better allocated. However, due to the transformation of government functions, there are some problems in the market-oriented mechanism of China's public service supply. For example, the main responsibility of providing public services is unclear. At present, the main bodies of providing public services in China are the government, enterprises and non-governmental organizations, and there is no clear division of labor among the three main bodies. Too much commitment by the government to the public service content that the market should undertake, or the competition phenomenon driven by interests, can easily lead to the absence and offside of public service supply.

In terms of government demand, with the expansion and differentiation of government organizational structure and the growingly complicated government affairs, the government is increasingly dependent on digital government services. The development and application of digital government services have solved the difficulties in many aspects, such as simplifying government procedures, reducing administrative costs, improving work efficiency, improving operation mechanism, changing organizational structure, coordinating departmental functions, etc., which makes the government see the sun again.

(2) Public demand

Since the reform and opening up, Chinese society has undergone historic changes: from the perspective of per capita income, from the starting point of 1978, when per capita GDP was only 155 US dollars, in 2010, per capita GDP exceeded 4200 US dollars, breaking the World Bank's upper middle income standard of 3945 US dollars, and the lower middle income group ranks among the upper middle income. From the perspective of per capita consumption expenditure, the per capita consumption expenditure of the national residents in 2020 was 21,210 yuan, down 1.6% from the previous year, and the Engel coefficient of the national residents was 30.2%, including 29.2% in cities and towns and 32.7% in rural areas. From the perspective of education level, in 2020, 1.107 million students will be enrolled in postgraduate education, 9.675 million students in ordinary colleges, 6.447 million students in secondary vocational education and 8.764 million students in ordinary high schools.

The consolidation rate of nine-year compulsory education is 95.2%, and the gross enrollment rate in high schools is 91.2%. In terms of the scale of Internet users, as of December 2020, the scale of Internet users in China reached 989 million, and the Internet penetration rate reached 70.4%.

Maslow's hierarchy of needs theory points out that, as shown in Fig. 6.1, people's needs are divided into low-level and high-level needs, and from low to high, they are divided into physiological and safety needs. When the low-level needs are met, they will pursue high-level needs, and the satisfied needs have less incentive for people, while the unsatisfied needs have greater incentive for people. With the continuous improvement of material life and spiritual life, great changes have taken place, and the public demand for government services has also changed.

On the one hand, the public expects the public services provided by the government to go beyond the physiological level and the security level to meet their social, respectful and self-fulfilling needs. On the other hand, the government is used to providing "equal treatment" services. It thinks that such public services are convenient and efficient, thus ignoring the individual needs of the public. As far as individual needs are concerned, it is difficult or even impossible to meet them in the traditional paper age. Practice shows that the introduction and wide application of e-government has changed this embarrassing situation. Taking online service and one-stop service of e-government system as examples, online service realizes the electronization, networking and intelligence of government affairs processing, while "one-stop service" realizes the centralization, flow and humanization of government affairs processing. Almost all individual demands of the public can

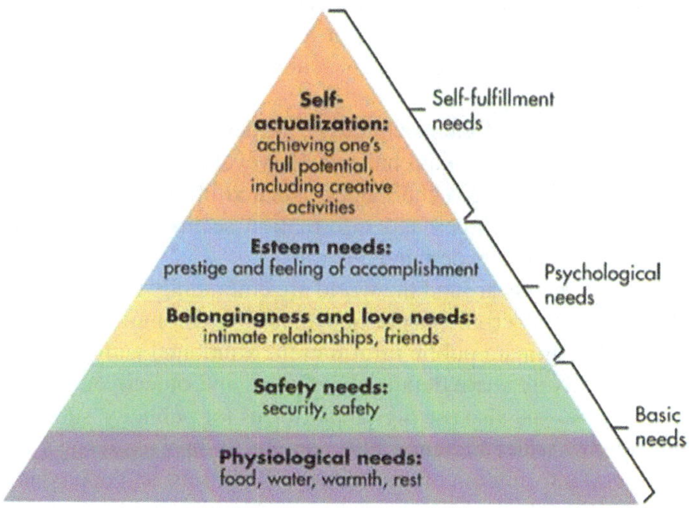

Fig. 6.1 Maslow's hierarchy of needs theory model

be processed by the "intelligent center" of e-government system and output corresponding results. Administrators often only need to do some auxiliary work in the process of government affairs realization.

6.1.2 Digital Technology

In the information age, digital technology and its subsidiary achievements are increasingly becoming the key carrier and core driving force for the development and progress of e-government. Although China's digital government service originated in the middle and late twentieth century, its great potential was not realized until the early twenty-first century, mainly due to the popularization and use of information technology such as Internet. No matter abroad or at home, every turning point and every leap is closely related to technical factors without any exception. In a sense, technology has become the decisive factor in the development of digital government services.

The development of digital technology has promoted the migration of government offline business to online digital space. Compared with the government office with complex business process, alienation from the public and paper office in the traditional business environment, this new business processing method not only improves the government's work efficiency, but also promotes the reform of examination and approval integration, and improves the convenience of enterprises' business to the public. Undoubtedly, relying on the new generation of information technologies such as 5G, artificial intelligence and big data, government governance will be promoted in a wider scope, at a deeper level and at a higher level. Social governance and economic development will be promoted to achieve quality change, efficiency change and power change.

With the development of digital technology, the demand of citizens and enterprises for digital government services has changed. However, the traditional e-government system is faced with four major challenges: isolated information island, redundant construction, scattered resources and information security, which makes it more difficult to cope with this new demand.

Therefore, governments around the world are embracing digital technology more and more. Many local governments use information and communication technology to publicize and disseminate public information. Municipal authorities use government websites to actively share details about plans and objectives, daily operations and service provision, and also use digital platforms for publicity, such as promoting local tourism among a wider audience. For example, Sydney has set up a data center to provide the general information of maps, data descriptions and open data sets to the public, covering multiple dimensions such as environment, community, economy, public domain, transportation, sustainability and culture. The Amman Municipal Government launched an updated electronic bidding platform in 2019, listing all local and international procurement opportunities and bidding application opportunities for municipal projects/contracts, aiming at managing and controlling the bidding procedures in a completely transparent manner and providing fair opportunities for investors.

During the COVID-19 outbreak, digital technology showed its superior application ability, which made knowledge spread rapidly, connected the government with the people, and maintained the operation of economy and society. During the epidemic period, the official website of the city provided relevant information to guide people to use the services related to COVID-19 provided by the central government, and publicly disseminated reliable information to raise people's awareness and connect people with appropriate resources. For example, the government of New South Wales, Australia developed a bulletin board to display the number of confirmed cases and provide community resources according to zip codes.

With the blockade of cities, new demands appear. For example, automatic chat robots play an important role in providing information to citizens. Singapore has launched a chat robot to keep users abreast of the latest developments in novel coronavirus. The parish of Jerva in Estonia has developed a community participation application in which local governments can share timely and reliable information and guidelines to prevent the spread of coronavirus. The application also includes a social interaction part, through which people can give feedback to local government officials, and can also post social trends and share pictures or videos. The municipal government of Sofia, Bulgaria, has also launched an application, through which citizens can report violations of quarantine requirements to support police work. An electronic platform has been deployed in the municipal government of Jimaraní s, Portugal, to register and manage volunteers who support the basic medical needs of the society, especially the vulnerable groups.

With residents isolated and many government employees working remotely, cities put more daily services on the Internet. To reduce the spread of bacteria in parking meters, New York encourages all residents and tourists to use the app to pay for parking fees. Many cities, such as Agra in India, have introduced remote video consultation facilities for electronic doctors, which has become one of the solutions to reduce indoor visits. Patients can consult online by mobile phone and download prescriptions offline.

Many cities also make use of their smart city infrastructure, and then use more advanced technologies to quickly respond to the epidemic. Public officials rely on real-time action, traffic or safety information to make information-based decisions and early crisis prediction, and adjust strategies accordingly. London uses cameras, sensors and artificial intelligence algorithms, which are usually used to control traffic, to measure the distance between pedestrians, so as to monitor whether people keep a social distance. London also uses liquidity data to predict changes in local security needs and measure changes in behavior after the blockade.

Digital technology provides a means for people to obtain mobile licenses through short messages, online applications or platforms to implement isolation measures, so that governments of various countries can make quick decisions based on real-time data and their analysis, and improve the coordination ability of governments. However, we should also realize that the development of digital technology will also bring disadvantages such as spreading false or doubtful information. How should we speed up the construction of digital government in the post-epidemic era? It has become a key issue that the government needs to focus on to improve service efficiency.

6.2 Digital Government Services for Doing-Digital-Business Environment Assessment

Since the new century, thanks to the development of big data, cloud computing, "internet plus" and other technologies, governments and their subordinate departments have realized the great potential of digital government in future governance. They concentrate the attention on accurately grasping the development dividend of information technology and the new ecology in the digital age, and the digital transformation of various government elements and the integration of traditional offline governance and online governance based on digital government services, in order to innovate governance concepts and methods. China is vigorously promoting the construction of "digital government". The construction of "digital government" breaks through the traditional business line vertical operation and single-department internal circulation mode, taking management, service, coordination and support as functional lines, and taking business environment, ecological civilization, urban operation, people's livelihood security, administrative efficiency and public support as business lines, and building a vertical and horizontal integrated "digital government" business system. The construction contents in the business environment mainly include three aspects: one is the construction of digital government service platform, the other is the construction of government portal website, and the third is the construction of new government media.

The digital government service platform mainly includes:

(i) The government service processing platform, namely the core business acceptance system, which implements the whole process online processing after the comprehensive acceptance of online government service matters, such as the general government service processing system and departmental business processing system;
(ii) Unified basic services on government service public support platform, such as online payment, identity authentication, electronic signature, unified message, security check, etc., to realize the integrated call of each upper business system;
(iii) Government service management platform, which is a platform for government service management departments at all levels to carry out government service management and manage government service matters in the whole province. It belongs to the background configuration of government service network and provides effective support for government affairs operation.

Government portals also are called government service networks of provinces, cities and counties, such as "Zhejiang Government Service Network". Its role is to unify the entrance, summarize the service information and government service columns of governments at all levels, and achieve scene-based work, and support people to make online appointments, apply online, pay online and inquire online. Its core business includes:

(i) Online service hall, which involves the opening of government affairs service (individual and legal person), government affairs disclosure, department window, government affairs supervision, public data resources and other information;
(ii) The network-run system, which can be simply understood as the background, mainly realizing the functions of service guide, service guide, service reservation, unified declaration, unified feedback, unified inquiry, unified evaluation and so on;
(iii) Service evaluation system, in which the public can make a unified evaluation of the staff and work efficiency through good bad reviews, so as to achieve all-round evaluation before, during and after the event, and offering the supervisor effective assess to the service department through evaluation;
(iv) multi-channel service, such as building government service network, WeChat applet, Alipay applet, APP, self-service terminal, telephone hotline, etc.

New media of government affairs, specifically refers to the government administrative organs at all levels and relevant functional units opening accounts or building their own platforms on third-party platforms such as Weibo, Tik Tok, WeChat, and Bilibili, releasing information, guiding public opinion, and contacting the masses to achieve the goal of building a service-oriented government and transforming government functions.

(i) Government Weibo, such as "safe Beijing", "Shanghai release", "Chinese meteorological science popularization", etc.;
(ii) Government WeChat, such as entering the "Guangzhou Public Security" WeChat official account, in which we can not only understand the police dynamics, but also have the functions of inquiring about car violations, account migration, immigration and other functions, and strive to meet the needs of the public;
(iii) Short videos of government affairs, such as lack of online celebrity accounts with over one million fans and nearly ten million praises, such as "Beijing SWAT", "China Changan Net" and "Jiangsu Net Police".

It can be seen that the development of digital government service platform, government website and new government media can fully show the current digital government service level in China. Therefore, in the evaluation of digital government service level for China's digital business environment, we mainly inspect the level of digital government service platform, the development of government websites, the development of new government media and so on, covering four measurable secondary indicators: the completeness of service mode, the coverage of service items, the accuracy of service guide and the maturity of online processing.

The completeness of service mode refers to the overall situation of the access mode provided by the digital government service platform, whether the enterprise can find the required service conveniently, quickly and accurately on the digital government service platform, and whether it supports WeChat applet, etc. The coverage of service items refers to the coverage of government affairs provided by digital government services, which is measured by the standardized combing and publication of the list of items and service guides displayed on the digital government platform. The accuracy of the service guide refers to the accuracy of the promotion and dissemination of digital government affairs, which is measured by the accuracy, detail and ease of use of the information of the service guide elements published on the digital government platform, government Weibo and government WeChat. The maturity of online processing focuses on the business process of digital government affairs, which is comprehensively measured by the number of days of digital government affairs service process, the number of transit events, and the favorable or poor evaluation of government affairs services.

6.3 Best Practices of Digital Government Services in China

(1) Xiong'an new area, Hebei, China

Xiong'an new area, Hebei Province, a national new district under the jurisdiction of Hebei Province, is located in the central part of Hebei Province, in the hinterland of Beijing, Tianjin and Baoding. Xiong'an new area includes Xiong County, Rongcheng County and Anxin County and some surrounding areas. The initial area is about 100 km^2. The medium-term development area is about 200 km^2. The long-term control area is about 2000 km^2, and the resident population is 1,047,100 (2017 data). On April 1, 2017, the Central Committee of the Communist Party of China and the State Council issued a notice deciding to set up a national new district, Xiong'an new area, Hebei Province. In 2018, the total investment scale of Xiong'an new area is about 300 billion yuan, mainly focusing on infrastructure construction and industrial development. Among them, more than 230 billion yuan of investment is concentrated in infrastructure construction such as railways, highways, drainage, ecological restoration, demolition and resettlement, etc. In 2019, the GDP of Xiong'an new area was 21.5 billion yuan. In the first three quarters of 2020, Xiong'an new area's investment in fixed assets increased by 16.6 times year-on-year, driving Hebei's investment growth by 3.3 percentage points.

As a national-level new district, Xiong'an government has bravely tried digital government affairs and accumulated rich practical experience.

First, actively promote the reform of "distribution suits". In order to promote the informatization construction of various departments and use informatization means to carry out government affairs work, a government information resource sharing platform and an integrated government service platform have been actively constructed. With the promotion work of the "one network management" of government service, Hebei Province covers 51 provincial departments, 13 municipal departments, Xiong'an new area, 191 counties (districts), 2269 townships (streets) and 49,968 villages (communities). The online handling rate of government affairs at provincial level in Hebei is as high as 91.16%. At the same time, the unified government affairs mobile terminal "Ji Shi Ban" is promoted to reach the mobile APP, the small program in WeChat and Alipay.

Second, promote the construction of "one center + four platforms" information infrastructure. Xiong'an takes supercomputing cloud data center as the carrier, Internet of Things platform, city CIM platform and video network platform as the convergence platform of urban spatial data and perceptual data, and block data platform as the underlying data platform, and launches the information infrastructure public platform system of "one center + four platforms", aiming at gathering government data, social data and urban three-dimensional spatial data, and realizing the underlying integration and authorized sharing of various data of urban production, life and operation.

Third, actively carry out the practice of new technology application. Xiong'an regards innovative technologies and the application practice of developing new technologies as successful experiences, laying a foundation for the high-quality development of digital economy in the future. At the same time, it also promotes the development of new industries, new formats and new models, and becomes a model for the future digital economy. The first thing we should do is to promote the application of blockchain. Xiong'an takes the management of relocation funds and engineering construction funds as the breakthrough point, comprehensively exploring the application innovation and technological innovation of blockchain in fund management to form a multi-chain collaborative blockchain technology system. In 2020, Xiong'an was approved to get the access to nearly 100 billion yuan of funds using the blockchain system. The second thing is to promote the application of electronic contracts. Based on the application of blockchain, it is estimated that all 54 projects and thousands of contracts built by Xiong'an will be in electronic form. And then the first thing is to carry out the application practice of digital identity and digital currency. At present, Xiong'an is jointly developing digital identity with the Ministry of Public Security, with a total of 294 bytes. It is planned to take the lead in the early practical application of Xiong 'an construction workers. On this basis, digital currency will be distributed to some workers to go forward the first step. And the last task we should focus on is to actively develop intelligent transportation. Xiong'an new area will gather the resources of operators, Internet companies, car companies, equipment manufacturers and other parties to jointly study the new intelligent development path of car intelligence, road intelligence and car-road collaboration. In the future, the share of bus travel field in Xiong'an will account for 80% of the total.

(2) Binhai New Area, Tianjin, China

Binhai New Area is a municipal district, a sub-provincial district, a national new district and a national comprehensive reform pilot area in Tianjin, China. It is located in the eastern coastal area of Tianjin and the center of the Bohai Economic Circle, with a total area of 2270 km^2 and a resident population of 2.99 million. It is the gateway to opening up to the outside world in North China, a high-level modern manufacturing and transformation base, an international shipping center and an international logistics center in the north, and a livable ecological new city. It is known as "the third growth pole of China's economy".

In March 1994, Tianjin decided to build Binhai New Area on the basis of Tianjin Economic and Technological Development Zone and Tianjin Port Free Trade Zone. In 2005, Binhai New Area was written into the Eleventh Five-Year Plan and incorporated into the national development strategy, and became a national-level new area with key support for development and opening up in China. On December 12, 2014, Binhai New Area was approved as the first free trade zone in North China.

Relying on the construction of smart city and digital government, Tianjin Binhai New Area is guided by big platform, big data, big system and great inheritance, and takes the opportunity of undertaking industrial transfer in the process of Beijing-Tianjin-Hebei integration to comprehensively promote the digital transformation of the traditional business environment.

First, improve the digital level of the government and build a safe and reliable government network platform. In order to promote the enterprise construction of government affairs informatization in the whole city, Binhai New Area issued a certified management method in 2019, and built a unified government affairs cloud platform in the way of purchasing services, providing unified computing and storage resources. At the same time, Tianjin's government extranet construction is also in the forefront of the country. At present, it is linked to the national extranet, and linked to the community or village, and then achieved four hundred percent. The municipal budget unit covers 100%. The administrative district covers 100%. And then the street community covers it. The optical cable of the whole network reaches 67,000 km. In addition, in terms of security, the backbone nodes of the municipal extranet are deployed with probes to realize real-time docking with the monitoring platform of the extranet, and an attack on the extranet from all over the world can be seen in real time.

Second, build a "1 + 4 + N" new smart city system, and comprehensively improve the intelligent level of Binhai New Area in various fields of economy and society. Tianjin Binhai New Area has realized 'big data perceives the city with one map', 'big platform, one network benefits people's livelihood' and 'big operation, one chain service industry'. The '1' in the '1 + 4 + N' system of Smart Binhai refers to the city brain of Smart Binhai, which uses the city operation and management center as the carrier to gather the data scattered in every corner of the city, open up information islands, break down departmental barriers and realize data sharing and intercommunication. It integrates the functions of city comprehensive management, convenience service response, emergency collaborative command and data research and development. Through the analysis and integration of a large number of data, it realizes accurate analysis, overall judgment and collaborative command of cities, supports the sustainable development of smart cities, and realizes a new generation of urban digital governance. '4' means focusing on four smart sectors, namely smart government affairs, smart economy, smart city and smart people's livelihood. 'N' refers to the intelligent application continuously developed according to the needs of urban management.

At present, the smart coastal project has covered four major sectors of government affairs, economy, city and people's livelihood, and has launched more than 30 specific applications. Among them, the application of the government service platform, the 'double service' system, and the global supervision platform for hazardous chemicals have achieved remarkable results: the total number of pieces handled by the government service platform exceeds 360,000, and the commercial registration system has reduced the length of pieces handled to 4 h, which is as high as 96.7% compared with the national standard length of 5 days. The monitoring platform of hazardous chemicals realizes the closed-loop monitoring and disposal of the whole process of production, transportation, storage and emergency disposal of hazardous chemicals in the whole region by collecting the data of emergency management, transportation and public security departments in real time. The Smart Coastal Project has also created a '15-min convenience service circle', so that the demands of the masses can be investigated and processed within 15 min to improve the efficiency of government services. The unified service mobile terminal 'Binhai Pocket Travel' can realize the unified acceptance, closed-loop management and full-process supervision of cross-level (district, street, community), cross-domain (people's livelihood, government affairs, economy, urban management) and inter-departmental urban operation events. All services are handled only at one end, only on one network and at fingertips, and the satisfaction of the masses is as high as 94.5%.

Third, speed up the construction of new infrastructure. In June 2020, the first batch of "new infrastructure" projects started in Binhai New Area, and 14 key projects with a total investment of 13.9 billion yuan started construction in the new area. In 2020, Binhai New Area will arrange 122 new infrastructure projects with a total investment of 167.1 billion yuan. The new infrastructure projects started in the new district cover three major areas: information infrastructure, converged infrastructure, and innovative infrastructure, involving 5G networks, artificial intelligence, collaboration between vehicles and roads, smart coastal areas, smart transportation, smart ports, and smart logistics. For example, Tianjin Port has realized the remote control of 5G unmanned truck. In the test, the vehicle runs at a speed of 15 km/h in the port production area. The 5G network is in a stable state during driving, with an average end-to-end video delay of 160 ms, which is at the leading level in the industry, meeting the needs of port production and operation, and fully verifying the feasibility of the unmanned truck based on 5G network for normal operation in ports.

Behind the 5G application scenario in Tianjin Port, the 5G network construction in Binhai New Area has entered the "fast lane", which is a microcosm of the blueprint of "new infrastructure" in Binhai New Area. At present, the "new infrastructure" in Binhai New Area presses the fast-forward button, one end is connected with investment and industry, and the other end is connected with the escalating consumer market, providing an infrastructure system of digital transformation, intelligent upgrading and integration and innovation, driving the interconnection of high-end industries, and becoming a new kinetic energy for accelerating the cultivation of new economy, new industries and new formats and promoting high-quality development.

Chapter 7
Digital Talents

Abstract Based on the literature digitization theory and the concept of digital doing-business environment, we analyzed the fundamental and driving role of digital literature in optimizing doing-business environment from the perspective of human capital theory and digital dividend theory. This chapter summarized 'efficiency improving', 'innovation encouraging' and 'inclusiveness promoting' as three major mechanisms which can improves digital literature and benefits the forming of a fair, balanced, healthy and sustainable development environment for the digital economy. In the evaluation of the doing-business environment, we set out the relevant secondary indicators from three dimensions of digital talent support, digital innovation activity and digital talent education for measurement. And then, we researched Didi Employment Promotion Plan, Zhaopin Recruitment that focused on the construction of talent ecology, Tencent's deep transformation of production-education-research and Hengan Jiaxin, which advocates that the government introduces a mechanism to attract talents.

7.1 Concept of Digital Literacy and Development of Digital Talents

7.1.1 Concept of Digital Literacy

With the advent of the digital economy era, digital ability has become an essential ability for individuals to adapt to their future work and life. International organizations such as OECD, World Economic Forum, World Bank and United Nations have identified digital ability as the basis in facing the ever-changing world in the future.[1] Digital ability refers to the ability to comprehensively use digital information technology to obtain returns (including economic returns, capacity growth, promotion of social participation, development opportunities, etc.), which means

[1] Wang Xuyan. Future-oriented Global Digital Literacy and Competency Standards Framework—An Analysis based on the "DQ Global Standards Report 2019" [J]. Library Development, 1–14 [2020-11-17].

X. Li et al., *Development Practice of Digital Business Environment in China*, Applied Economics and Policy Studies,
https://doi.org/10.1007/978-981-16-8527-9_7

that individuals can use enough skills and abilities to accomplish social tasks efficiently, not covering the cognitive ability to express creative ideas, attitudes towards social development, culture and ethics, and other advanced abilities. Digital competence is generally regarded as a part of digital literacy, and "literacy" is regarded as a holistic concept, constantly changing and advancing with the times. It is an advanced capability element system including digital competence.[2]

The term "digital literacy" first appeared in 1994, and Israeli scholar Y. Eshet-Alkalai summarized it as "the ability to understand and use various digital resources and information displayed by computers".[3] Then Paul Gilster formally put forward the concept of "Digital Literacy" for the first time in his book *Digital Literacy*. He defined digital literacy as the ability to acquire, understand and integrate digital information, including skills such as web search, hypertext reading, digital information criticism and integration, and described digital literacy as the use and understanding of information in the digital age. He also emphasized the importance of digital technology as a "basic life skill", and then distinguished digital literacy from traditional printing reading and writing skills.[4]

Obviously, digital literacy is not a single skill, but a complex and interdisciplinary open literacy, which can promote individuals to acquire a variety of survival skills including digital ability, enhance the creative cognitive ability of social groups and become an important asset for the development of information society. Academic circles agree on the importance of digital literacy in personnel training in the twenty-first century, but the definition of digital literacy framework and concept has been confused. Relevant research shows that there are more than 100 models and frameworks of digital literacy at present, but there is no one framework model universally recognized at present. Most framers consider their own political, economic and social environment, but there are regional differences in digital literacy framework. It shows the characteristics of cross-country and cross-organization. There are always different countries and international organizations constantly trying to formulate a unified standard digital literacy framework.[5]

The most influential researches on digital literacy in the world mainly include twenty-first century Skills of the United States and Key Competences of the European Union, which especially has a profound influence on the subsequent research on digital literacy. As one of the eight core qualities emphasized by the European Union, digital literacy has experienced a conceptual change from the initial "information technology" (emphasizing technology itself) to "information technology skills and use", "information technology skills" (emphasizing use skills) and "digital literacy"

---

[2] Wang Youmei, Yang Xiaolan, Hu Wei & Wang Juan. Conception Continuum, System Elements and Integrated Model: From Digital Literacy to Digital Competence [J]. Journal of Distance Education, 2013, 31(03):24–29.

[3] Wang Junmin, Huang Yuesheng, Shen Yayun. Research Status and Enlightenment of Digital Literacy [J]. Digital Education, 2018, 4(01):15–21.

[4] Gilster P. Digital Literacy [M]. New York: Wiley, 1997: 25–48.

[5] Mark Brown. The challenge of digital literacy: Beyond narrow skills to critical mindsets.

(emphasizing literacy),[6] which is defined by the European Union as "the ability to use information technology confidently, critically and innovatively in work, employment, study, leisure and social participation". It emphasized that people interact and cooperate on the basis of information acquisition and use. The EU "Digital Literacy Project" was implemented in 2011, setting three goals. The first one is to determine the core elements that affect digital literacy. The second one is to improve the EU digital literacy framework/indicators on the basis of previous studies. And the third one is to propose a digital literacy framework applicable to all citizens. The digital literacy framework proposed by the project includes five literacy domains: information, communication, content creation, security awareness and problem solving, as shown in Table 2.1. Each literacy domain is extended to a number of "specific Competences" indicators, which are divided into three "profitability levels": A\B\C. A is "basic", B is "medium", and C is "advanced", which are defined from three dimensions: knowledge, skills and attitude.

7.1.2 Development of Digital Talents

Digital talents refer to talents with ICT (Information and Communication Technology) professional skills and supplementary skills, and are the people who can use digital skills to obtain certain economic benefits among netizens. That is to say, the foundation of digital talents comes from a group of people who can use digital networks. According to the 47th Statistical Report on Internet Development in China, as of December 2020, the number of Chinese Internet users was 989 million, accounting for about 20% of the global Internet users. During the "Thirteenth Five-Year Plan" period, the scale of Internet users in China increased by 43.7% in the past five years, and the trend that the growth subjects changed from youth groups to minors and elderly groups became increasingly obvious. Minors and "silver-haired" elderly groups surfed the net one after another, which constituted China's pluralistic and huge digital society. From the perspective of the attribute structure of netizens, as of December 2020, the ratio of male to female netizens in China is 51:49, which is basically consistent with the ratio of male to female in the overall population. Among them, netizens aged 20–29, 30–39 and 40–49 accounted for 17.8%, 20.5% and 18.8% respectively, and netizens with junior high school, high school/technical secondary school education were 40.3% and 20.6% respectively. Only 9.3% of netizens have the bachelor degree or above. From the perspective of academic structure, there are obvious shortage of high-end digital talents.

Talent is the carrier of technology and the foundation of innovation. The essential characteristics of innovation-driven development determine that digital talent is the core driving factor of the development of digital economy. With more and more countries and regions speeding up the layout of digital economy and striving to seize

[6] Ren Youqun, Sui Xiaoxiao, Liu Xinyang. On the Framework of EU Digital Competence [J]. Modern Distance Education Research, 2014(05):3–12.

the opportunities in the digital age, the global demand for typical digital talents with computer science, software engineering, artificial intelligence, data science and electronic engineering as the background is growing rapidly.

According to "Current Situation and Prospects of Digital Talents in China 2020", the overall demand for digital talents in the market soared after the epidemic, which increased by 91% compared with the same period of last year. The demand for digital talents in IT Internet was far ahead, accounting for 80% of the whole industry, followed by education and training industry, manufacturing industry, communication electronics and financial industry. The integration of traditional fields and the Internet requires a large number of professional and technical personnel to explore the integration technology and build the underlying architecture. The demand for digital professionals in these industries is generally higher than that of the other two types of talents. Real estate construction, financial industry and other industries have the most urgent demand for digital leadership reform, and the demand for digital management talents is stronger. Manufacturing, education and training, communications and electronics, and transportation and logistics industries have a stronger demand for digital application talents. These industries are seeking digital integration at the business level, and there are more digital business scenarios.

At present, the ratio of supply and demand of digital professionals in China is seriously unbalanced, and the quality of talents has a tremendous shortage to meet the requirements of industrial development. No matter the academic qualifications, majors or technical experience, it poses a clear and precise challenge to the digital professional skills of talents.

7.2 The Mechanism of Improving the Digital Literacy of the Population for Optimizing the Doing-Digital-Business Environment

7.2.1 The Position of Population Digital Literacy in the Construction of Doing-Digital-Business Environment

(1) Improving the human capital of doing-digital-business is the foundation of building a doing-digital- business environment.

From the perspective of human capital theory, talents with digital literacy provide high-quality human capital for digital business. The new economic theory holds that human capital is a key factor in analyzing economic growth by endogenous growth model, and emphasizes that the production of human capital is more important than the production of material capital. Scholars at home and abroad have three main understandings of the mechanism of human capital acting on economic growth. First, they regard human capital as the input factor of final product production and directly act on economic growth. Second, they regard human capital as the key input of technological production and indirectly act on economic growth by using innovation and technological diffusion. Third, they regard human capital as both the input factor of final product and the key input of technological production. It is a joint mechanism.[7]

For the digital economy, we also tend to think that the population with digital literacy is also a joint mechanism for promoting the growth model of the digital economy. On the one hand, the population with digital literacy directly acts on the digital economy as the input factor of the final product production. The digital economy marked by the new generation of digital technologies such as blockchain, cloud computing, big data, AI, and digital twins needs to have the above technologies and the people with these skills will create economic value through digital production. On the other hand, the population with digital literacy, as the key input of technology production, indirectly affects the digital economy through knowledge application and technology diffusion in the production process. They influence the development of the digital economy by influencing technological progress. The promotion of total factor productivity in digital economy mainly depends on technological innovation and diffusion and absorption of cutting-edge science and technology, and the stock of human capital greatly affects these two aspects. The more people with high-quality digital literacy, the faster the speed of knowledge innovation and technology diffusion, and the more obvious the corresponding human capital can promote the growth of productivity in digital economy.

Obviously, the starting point and foothold of building a doing-digital-business environment are to protect the development of digital economy. Through the above analysis of the mechanism of population digital literacy for digital economic growth in human capital theory, we can see that the population with digital literacy is an important human capital and a key driver for the development of digital economy.

(2) It is conducive to the full release of digital dividends and is the key driving force for the construction of a digital business environment

Digital dividend refers to the extensive benefits brought by using digital technologies (including the Internet, mobile phones and all other tools for collecting, storing, analyzing and sharing information by digital means),[8] mainly including three aspects: economic growth, employment increase and service improvement. The digital literacy of the population affects the digital dividend release by influencing the absorption and diffusion of digital technology, thus exerting an effect on the digital business environment.

[7] Du Wei, Yang ZhiJiang, Xia Guoping. Study on the Impact Mechanism of Human Capital on Economic Growth [J]. China Soft Science, 2014(08):173–183.

[8] World Bank Group. World Bank Development Report: Digital Dividends [R]. The World Bank, 2016.

First of all, digital literacy plays a positive role in promoting the absorption of digital technology knowledge. The premise of diffusion and commercial application of a digital technology is that some people use it. However, different people have different preferences for knowledge absorption. People who have never been exposed to computer-related knowledge are inefficient in absorbing digital technology knowledge, while people with certain digital literacy are efficient in absorbing digital technology knowledge. They can combine their own digital knowledge reserves to summarize and sort out the absorbed knowledge, and it is very possible to research and produce new technologies and new knowledge, so as to complete the transformation and upgrading of the existing digital technology knowledge system.

Secondly, digital literacy plays a key role in the process of digital technology diffusion and iterative innovation. The diffusion model of digital technology basically follows the diffusion model of ICT technology and Rogers' innovation diffusion, showing an "S" curve as a whole, as shown in Fig. 3.2. In the "O-A" stage, which is the earliest stage of the emergence of technology 1, a necessary condition is that someone will use this technology first and spread the skills. With the increase of the number of users (digital skill owners) of this technology, technology 1 gradually spreads, but the spread speed is slow; With the increasing number of people with digital skills of technology 1, technology 1 has entered a period of rapid development, that is, the "A-B" period in the picture; When the number of users of technology 1 reaches a certain proportion in the total population, that is, the number of people with this digital skill reaches saturation, the development of technology 1 enters a stagnant and slow-down period. At this time, the number of users can no longer provide power for the development of digital technology, and it can only rely on the population with this digital skill to innovate knowledge, improve the literacy in the digital literacy domain such as information, knowledge exchange, content creation and problem solving, and develop new technology (technology 2) through iterative innovation. It can be seen that the digital literacy of the population is a breakthrough point in the transformation from old technology to new technology, and plays a key driving role in the iterative innovation of digital technology (Fig. 7.1).

7.2.2 Promoting the Digital Literacy of the Population to Optimize the Doing-Digital-Business Environment

Through the theoretical analysis of digital literacy and doing-digital-business environment above, three boosting mechanisms for improving population digital literacy to build digital business environment are summarized. The first one is to improve efficiency to optimize digital production environment including digital infrastructure environment, data security environment, competition and consumer protection environment, supervision and service environment. The second one is to promote innovation to stimulate innovation vitality of digital innovation environment. And

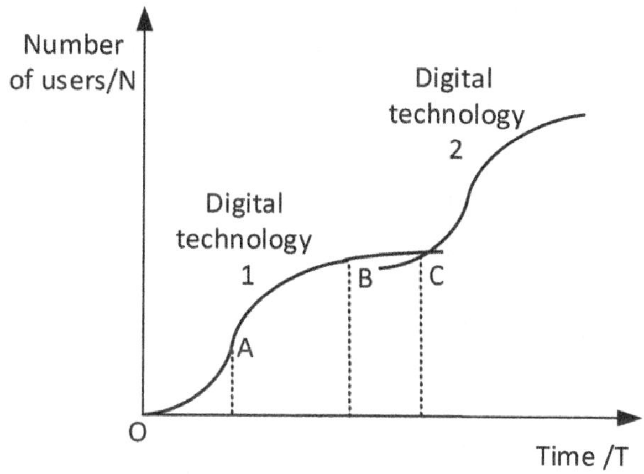

Fig. 7.1 Digital technology diffusion model

the third one is to promote inclusion to create a fair, balanced, healthy and sustainable development environment, as shown in Fig. 7.2.

(1) To improve efficiency to optimize the digital production environment

Improving the digital literacy of the population can obviously improve the human capital in the doing-digital-business environment, and the total factor production efficiency of the digital production environment including the digital infrastructure environment, data security environment, competition and consumer protection environment, and supervision and service environment. Human capital is an important factor of production that can't be ignored in any economic form. Especially in the

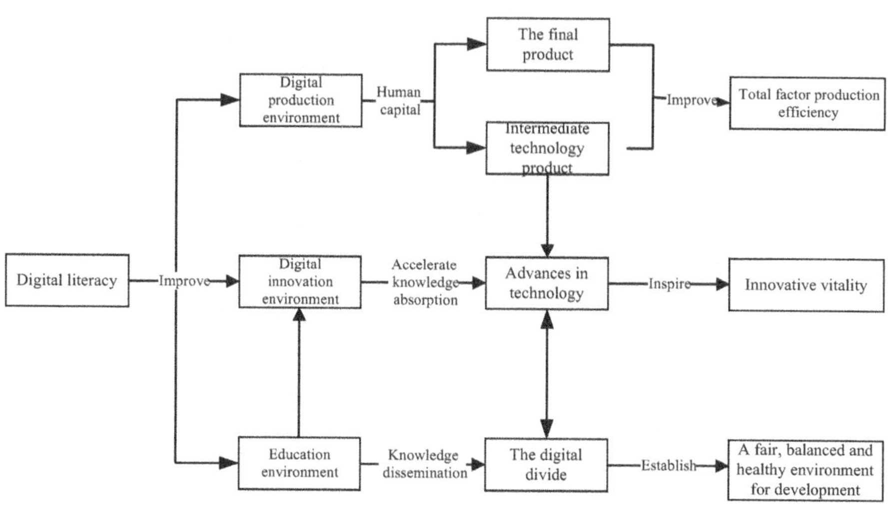

Fig. 7.2 The boosting mechanism of improving the digital literacy of the population to optimize the digital business environment

development of digital economy, which emphasizes digital innovation, high-quality human capital can be used as an input factor of final products to improve the production efficiency and product value of final products. It can also be used as an input factor of intermediate technology products to promote technological progress, improve total factor production efficiency and promote the growth of digital economy, and optimize the digital production environment.

(2) Pushing innovation to enhance the vitality of innovation and activate the digital innovation environment

Improving population's digital literacy can accelerate the absorption and diffusion of digital technology, promote technological progress and stimulate the innovation vitality of digital innovation environment. Technological change based on digital information and communication technology (ICT) is an important driving force for the progress of social informatization. At the same time, it constantly drives the multi-dimensional innovation of the whole society and multi-fields, including technological innovation, product and service innovation, organizational innovation and institutional innovation, so as to realize the allocation of resources in the economic environment and improve the efficiency of economic operation. The wide application of digital technology in the fields of production, finance, scientific research and education, medical care, enterprise and government management, and family and personal social life has had a huge and profound impact on economic and social development, and fundamentally changed people's lifestyles, behaviors and values. A doing-business environment full of innovative vitality is conducive to the dissemination and accumulation of knowledge and technological innovation.

(3) Promoting inclusion to create a fair, healthy and sustainable development environment

The vigorous development of digital economy has continuously promoted the progress of modern society. However, the construction of information society is not achieved overnight, and the degree of diffusion and penetration of digital technology has never been uniform and undifferentiated. There is a "digital gap" among different countries, different regions, and people of different ages, occupations and genders, and with the further diffusion of technology, the digital gap is deepening.

In the early days, researchers and policy makers generally paid attention to the differences in ICT infrastructure access, that is, the differences between people who have access to ICT and those who have not. However, with the gradual popularization of Internet access in developed countries, especially the increasing popularity of broadband access, the differences in network use have become increasingly prominent. Because different people have different levels of mastering network application skills, their ability to effectively obtain and use information through the network is different, which is manifested in the differences in network use time, use intensity, behavior patterns, and information search efficiency. In recent years, Internet access has become highly popular in countries with leading ICT development, and the new digital divide is becoming increasingly significant. It has been observed that even if users can access ICT infrastructure independently and without restrictions, there are obvious differences in their proficiency in accomplishing specific tasks and achieving specific goals by using the network. Even if users have the same skill level and achieve the same use intensity, the returns (including economic returns, capacity growth, social participation improvement, development opportunities, etc.) that can be obtained from network use are often different,[9] and even very different, that is, the difference of users' digital literacy brings a new digital divide.

Improving the population's digital literacy can make ordinary people more sensitive and receptive to digital knowledge, help spread knowledge, bridge the digital divide to a certain extent, and help optimize the educational environment. The relationship between education environment and digital literacy of talents is inseparable, which is a two-way relationship. Education can improve the digital literacy of population, which in turn can strengthen the education level through technical means. In recent years, developed countries have increased the digital literacy education for the population, such as the all-round citizen digital literacy training model in the United States,[10] and the United Kingdom has integrated personal digital literacy into the professional development education model.[11] At present, China is actively exploring the educational model of improving digital literacy.

7.3 Digital Literacy Training in Doing- Digital-Business Environment Assessment

The training of digital talents can make ordinary people more sensitive and receptive to digital knowledge. It helps spread knowledge, bridge the digital divide to a certain extent, and help optimize the educational environment. The relationship between education environment and digital literacy of talents is inseparable, and it is a two-way relation. Education can improve the digital literacy of population, which in turn can strengthen the education level through technical means. Therefore, the cultivation of digital talents plays a key role in optimizing the digital business environment, and digital literacy should be evaluated as a key indicator in the evaluation of doing-digital-business environment.

In many evaluation systems, there are related measures of digital literacy level, such as "Internet user skills" and "advanced skills and development" in Digital

[9] OECD. Understanding the digital divide.2001.

[10] Zhang Juan. The Current Situation and Enlightenment of American Digital Literacy Education [J]. Library and Information Service, 2018(6):135–142.

[11] Li Chunhui. Research on the Practice of Digital Literacy Education in UK University Libraries [J]. Library Development, 2017(8): 78–82.

Table 7.1 Indicators related to digital talents and innovation in the evaluation system of five international organizations

International organizations	Indicator name	First year date	Correlation measure index
ITU	ICT development index	2009	ICT skills (average years of education, total enrollment rate, proportion of people with ICT skills)
United Nations Conference on Trade and Development (UNCTAD)	E-commerce index	2014	Personal holding rate of financial institution account or mobile wallet
United Nations Department of Economic and Social Affairs	E-government survey	2011	Human Capital Index (HCI)
World Intellectual Property Organization (WIPO)	Global innovation index	2007	ICT and business model creation, ICT and organizational model creation
World economy tire	The global competitiveness index	2004	Digital skills, entrepreneurial risk attitude and financial system of professional population

Economy and Society Index (DESI) 2020,[12] 'ICT skills (average years of education, total enrollment rate, proportion of people with ICT skills)',[13] the "Human Capital Index" issued by the UN Department of Economic and Social Affairs, etc., as Table 7.1.

The above indicators can effectively measure the digital literacy level of the society, but they do not measure the effect of some government measures to support the training of digital talents. In the evaluation of the doing-digital-business environment, we should consider more the support and tolerance of the government and the society for the development of digital talents. Therefore, referring to the international secondary indicators of relevant evaluation indicators, we set out the relevant secondary indicators from the three dimensions of digital talent support, digital innovation activity and digital talent education for measurement.

[12] Basol O, Yalin E C. How Does the Digital Economy and Society Index (DESI) Affect Labor Market Indicators in EU Countries [J]. Human Systems Management, 2020, 39(1).

[13] International Telecommunication Union, The ICT Development Index (IDI): conceptual framework and methodology, https://www.itu.int/en/ITU-D/Statistics/Pages/publications/mis2017/methodology.aspx.

(1) Digital talent support

Digital talent support mainly measures the government's support for digital talents. First, the government's policies and measures to encourage digital talent innovation, including strategies, regulations, systems, financial and financing support policies or measures to support the transformation of achievements, platform construction, etc. The second one is about the digital talent system construction plan, implementation effect and digital human resources market service institutions.

(2) Digital innovation activity

Digital innovation activity mainly measures the active situation of digital talents in the digital economy field, and examines the innovation and entrepreneurship, achievements transformation and typical cases and practices in the digital economy field.

(3) digital talent education

Digital talent education mainly measures the society's training of digital talents, including strengthening the construction of new disciplines of digital economy in colleges and universities, personnel training institutions and human resources training institutions, etc.

7.4 Practice of Digital Talent Training in China in Recent Years

7.4.1 Didi Employment Promotion Plan

Didi Chuxing is the world's leading mobile travel platform, providing convenient and diversified travel services for 450 million users in more than 400 cities. At the same time, with Didi's digital transformation and upgrading of the traditional travel industry, the number of employment opportunities and employment patterns driven by Didi's travel have gradually extended to the whole industrial chain, bringing a brand-new employment system. Employment opportunities can be divided into two types: direct employment and indirect employment. Direct employment can also be divided into some countries along the belt and road initiative from the perspective of domestic and overseas, as shown in Table 7.2.

Didi provides flexible job and income opportunities for car owners, drivers and riders, and keeps paying attention to employment. On August 13, 2020, Didi announced that it would invest 200 million special funds to launch the "Orange-Italy" employment promotion plan to help more people achieve flexible employment through the platform. This plan includes such measures as 'promoting, helping, stabilizing and learning'. The "Orange Promotion" initiative will be used for the joining rewards, car rental subsidies, adaptation period income subsidies, insurance purchase subsidies, etc. for new drivers who join the network. The 'Orange Help' initiative will help difficult and special groups to work on the platform, such as special poverty

Table 7.2 Employment system of drip platform

Type	Types of platform employment opportunities	Representative platform business module	Mainly driving the form of employment
Direct employment	Didi platform itself is employed	Basic business construction of Didi platform	Direct employment (including outsourcing)
	Employment related to network car	Network car driver, leasing company	Online odd jobs and offline employment
	Employment related to inclusive business	Driving, green orange bicycle operation and maintenance, motorcycle operation and maintenance	Online odd jobs and offline employment
	Small orange car service related employment	Small orange car rental, small orange charging, small orange refueling, small orange car maintenance, etc.	Employment under the line
Drive employment indirectly	Automobile production and employment	Driven by the network car operating vehicles	Mainly for offline employment
Direct employment in countries along the belt and road initiative	Employment in overseas business	Overseas network car driver	Online odd jobs

alleviation for drivers in poverty-stricken areas to promote employment. The 'Orange Stability' initiative will set a three-month assistance period for newly joined network car drivers and give a number of free financial product support, including giving accident insurance. The 'range Learning' initiative will continue to provide skills training for people who work flexibly through the platform.

For the drivers of the stock network who can achieve flexible employment through the platform, Didi tries to increase the income opportunities of drivers in different time periods and different locations, and balance the work habits of different drivers. At the same time, Didi introduced more flexible car rental products such as 'rent at will', and provided drivers with preferential services such as charging, refueling and insurance, thus reducing the cost of drivers. With the promotion of drivers' grades, they will also get more welfare rights and growth channels.

According to Didi's travel, the flexible employment pattern represented by the drivers of online cars can play the role of 'reservoir', 'stabilizer' and 'charging treasure' for employment, and create flexible employment and income opportunities for more groups. According to the data, Didi Platform has driven more than 10 million flexible employment opportunities, including network drivers, driving masters and bike-sharing operation and maintenance personnel. Among them, there are more than 3000 leasing companies around ecology, which indirectly drives more than 6 million related jobs in the upstream and downstream of the industrial chain.

In addition, Didi signed an employment cooperation agreement with the Department of Veterans Affairs in 2020, providing more than 15,000 employment opportunities for veterans, including luxury car drivers and special car drivers. At the same time, Didi is also promoting employment to help the poor. Didi is actively participating in the 'Digital Platform Economy Promoting Employment and Helping Poverty Alleviation' sponsored by the Ministry of Human Resources and Social Security and the Poverty Alleviation Office of the State Council. As one of the main partners, Didi will provide sustainable platform employment opportunities for people in 52 poverty-stricken counties and help them get rid of poverty through employment. At the same time, Didi donated bike-sharing to poverty-stricken counties in need, and the operating income was used to set up public welfare posts in the local areas, helping the poor people who set up their cards to find jobs. In addition, Didi also joined the 'Famous Private Enterprises Traveling to Hubei' jointly sponsored by the All-China Federation of Industry and Commerce, Hubei Provincial People's Government and China Glory Business Promotion Association. This year, it will provide 8000 flexible employment opportunities in Hubei Province, such as network car drivers and two-wheeled vehicle operation and maintenance, to help local people stabilize employment and restore the economy.

Up to now, employment promotion training has been carried out in Qingdao and Yantai, credit system construction has been carried out, on-line drivers' word-of-mouth value evaluation has been carried out, and 318,000 people's applications have been rejected. During online operation, mutual evaluation between drivers and passengers is possible. Didi believes that information fusion can achieve greater value, and the credit data of government and enterprises can be integrated and applied, which can support security certification channels and break through the barriers of credit system construction.

7.4.2 Zhaopin Recruitment Focuses on the Construction of Talent Ecology

Since its establishment 26 years ago, Zhilian Recruitment Company has focused on the construction of talent ecology, with a market value of over 2.1 billion yuan, ranking first in the industry in terms of market scale. At present, there are 6000 employees and 39 branches, and the whole process of talent recruitment has been launched online, which lowers the threshold of employment and entrepreneurship.

(1) Committed to improving the service experience of the whole process of HR management

Based on years of experience in human resources service, Zhilian divides human resources management into ten key process nodes, such as 'selection, entry, use, retention, education, promotion, reduction, adjustment, resignation and separation', covering recruitment, training development, organization and management, performance incentive and other modules. In recent years, Zhilian is committed to improving the service experience of the whole process of HR management through several micro-innovations.

Zhaopin Recruitment is based on the deep insight into the recruitment service scene of enterprises, while iteratively optimizing the service experience on the PC side. In recent years, it has increased the investment on the mobile side, which is convenient for job hunting and recruitment to communicate with each other, as well as the horizontal cooperation between HR and hiring managers in enterprise recruitment. In order to solve the problem of collaboration efficiency between HR and employing department, Zhilian designed the collaboration function between employing manager and HR, employing department was responsible for setting standards and testing skills, while HR tracked the overall recruitment effect in an advisory way to improve recruitment efficiency and effectiveness. In the process of recruitment, enterprises can also release more subjective initiative, and the newly launched 'talent magnet' product can realize all-round initiative. 'Hook up' your favorite talents online at any time, and both parties can send resumes with one click, instead of blindly matching.

Like other industries, the traditional operation mode of human resources industry is being subverted, which will give a wide imagination under the blessing of technology. Only intelligent technology and mode innovation can quickly promote the 'qualitative change' in this field. The qualitative change is the commercial barrier that competitors can't surpass. Zhilian in the 5G era empowers people and opportunities in the ecology through AI, realizes accurate matching, and constantly enriches scenes around opportunities that can be realized, thus continuously deriving and transforming the value of human capital.

(2) Create an open human capital ecology and continuously expand the ecological boundary

We should know how to take off at the wind outlet. In the process of technology permeating all walks of life, enterprises with vision and foresight will not only focus on self-construction, but drive the whole industry to set sail. On the basis of creating an open human capital ecology, Zhilian Recruitment empowers partners in the upstream and downstream of the industrial chain to realize energy resonance. In recent years, it has successively invested in strategic partners such as 51 social security, Pulse and Ape Circle, incubating new species and expanding ecological boundaries.

Specifically, Zhilian's capital layout is still around the ecological chain. 51 social security is committed to providing social security services for small and medium-sized enterprises, helping Zhilian recruitment to further improve the value chain of enterprise service. The circle focuses on talent evaluation in the vertical field, improves the recruitment efficiency of programming positions, and helps Zhilian expand its service depth in the IT field. As the largest workplace social platform in real-name registration system in China, it has rich user-touching scenes, and its social attributes enhance stickiness, thus becoming the social extension of Zhilian.

Cross-border extension, most afraid of crazy expansion, leads to lack of energy in the main business, resulting in scattered business. Finally, the profits of the main business have to be used to make up for cross-border industries, which is also the primary reason why Wu Xiaobo summed up the failure of large enterprises in Big Defeat.

Zhilian, on the other hand, seems to have a wide investment field, but its focus is highly converged. Professional teams are incorporated into its own system. This series of internal and external actions make the brand image of Zhilian recruitment younger and more intelligent, paving the way for the future of Zhilian. Just like the main planet surrounded by satellites in the universe, it is the habit of Internet giants to incubate valuable projects and enterprises. Integrating the industrial chain is not only the result of strength, but also the need to strengthen its own industry status.

7.4.3 Tencent's Deep Transformation of Production, Education and Research

Shenzhen Tencent Computer System Co., Ltd. was established in November 1998. It was founded by Ma Huateng, Zhang Zhidong, Xu Chenye, Chen Yidan and Ceng Liqing. It is one of the largest Internet integrated service providers in China and one of the Internet enterprises with the largest number of service users in China. In view of the training of digital talents, Tencent believes that at present, Haidian Company should take advantage of universities and high-end talents, and introduce more innovative forms to realize the deep transformation of production, education and research. Second, more policies on science, technology and culture industries and talent service should be introduced to help enterprises retain and attract more sophisticated talents.

(1) Tencent Cloud holds hands with Zhejiang University to promote the integration of production, education and research

Tencent Cloud, as a public cloud platform for enterprises and individuals created by 0Tencent, relies on Tencent's Internet service capabilities in QQ, WeChat and other massive businesses for more than ten years to provide high-speed, stable and secure cloud services for games, video, finance, internet plus, e-commerce and other industries. In 2017, Tencent Cloud and Zhejiang University jointly listed "Zhejiang University Zijin Town Tencent Cloud Base", providing overall cloud services for cloud computing creation space and hatched projects in the town, and providing resource services of Tencent ecosystem. At the same time, Tencent Cloud provides cloud computing technology and solutions, and builds Tencent Cloud technology space and open laboratory. Strive to create a national-level space for professional creation, and explore a new mode of cooperation between universities and leading enterprises.

In terms of personnel training, the two sides will hold the 'CTO Class of Tencent Cloud Computing Institute', in which Tencent technical experts will provide targeted training to CTO of alumni enterprises of Zhejiang University and CTO of outstanding teams in the park. And create a systematic and comprehensive environment for entrepreneurs to accelerate their cultivation and incubation.

The cooperation between the two parties is dedicated to exploring new innovation mechanism and mode of industry-university-research cooperation, creating new innovation and entrepreneurship carriers, gathering relevant innovation and entrepreneurship resources at home and abroad, and promoting the close integration of technology research and development, venture capital and entrepreneurship incubation. Tencent Cloud will provide 'Cloud + Entrepreneurship' support plan to provide cloud resources support for high-quality startups, and provide Tencent Cloud technology and service docking support for enterprises and alumni enterprises in Zijin Town, Zhejiang University.

This cooperation is a good beginning for Tencent Cloud and universities to jointly build the integration mode of production, education and research. Hangzhou CTO training class is only the beginning. Tencent Cloud will also support more excellent start-up enterprises in universities in the future, and accelerate the practical application and industrialization of scientific research achievements in domestic universities.

(2) Tencent AI Lab and the Institute of Agricultural Information of Chinese Academy of Agricultural Sciences jointly established a joint laboratory for smart agriculture

As one of the Internet giants, Tencent, with first-class technology and talents, has been vigorously promoting cross-border research on cutting-edge technology and agriculture. At present, Tencent AI Lab and Information Institute of Chinese Academy of Agricultural Sciences have set up a joint laboratory for smart agriculture to explore interdisciplinary frontier research on the combination of agriculture and AI, IoT, big data, cloud computing and robots, and to create a smart solution in China. In addition, it has successively signed strategic agreements with COFCO, Guangdong Yuewang Agricultural Group, Shenzhen Yijiacang, zhongkai university of agriculture and engineering, etc., to carry out deep cooperation in smart agriculture from the industrial side, strategically lay out the agricultural Internet, and practice the integration of production, education and research.

In the future, the Smart Agriculture Joint Laboratory will focus on exploring the following two aspects.

First, combine the existing accumulation and national conditions, develop general artificial intelligence planting solutions in a controllable environment, and promote industrial upgrading and independent research and development of China's smart programs;

Second, based on algorithms, integrating the advantages of both sides in technology and agricultural knowledge, linking IoT, robotics, computer vision and other capabilities, looking for the combination of cutting-edge technology and modern agriculture, and cooperating to carry out original innovation.

7.4.4 Hengan Jiaxin Advocates that the Government Introduce a Scoring Mechanism to Attract Talents with a Points System

Hengan Jiaxin focuses on solving the security problems of communication network, next generation internet, industrial control network and other information systems. It has abundant technical reserves and strong innovation ability. It has owned a number of national patents and software copyrights in this field, and has established strategic partnerships with many well-known enterprises, key universities, national authorities and professional groups in the industry It is committed to providing reliable high-end services for national and enterprise infrastructure security and information security.

Since its establishment, Hengan Jiaxin has upgraded the construction of technological innovation system to the strategic height of the company's future development, constantly updating and iterating existing technologies and products, and researching and developing innovative technologies and products with industry influence. Based on years of research on basic security technology, Hengan Jiaxin has formed a core technology group including real-time processing technology of massive data integrating Internet and communication network, intelligent security engine technology with deep learning ability, 'cloud-network-edge-end' integrated management and control technology, etc., and an independent and controllable intellectual property system, as shown in Table 7.3.

Based on the technical products developed above, Hengan Jiaxin has offered a lot of support for the optimization of doing-digital-business environment, including industrial Internet security, public Internet security, cyber fraud and so on, which have released related products. From the perspective of enterprises, I hope that the government can provide a scoring mechanism for enterprises. For example, if some enterprises can participate in the construction of doing-digital-business environment, such an enterprise that can contribute to the environment will rely on the points system and tilt the policies of tax reduction, talent introduction and housing office space. It will provide some high-quality services to such enterprises participating in the construction of doing-digital-business environment through such a mechanism.

Table 7.3 Henganjia new technology product system

Core technology category	Name of core technology	Application field
Real-time processing technology of massive data integrated with internet and communication network	Integrated acquisition technology of internet and communication network	It can be applied to communication network data collection and analysis products, IDC security management products, communication network fraud protection products and communication network optimization products; In addition, it can also be applied to network quality monitoring, business performance optimization (APM) and other fields
	PB-level big data storage processing technology	It can be applied to communication network fraud protection products, security awareness and emergency management platforms, and communication network optimization products; It can also be applied to digital cities, intelligent transportation and other fields
Intelligent Security Engine Technology with Deep Learning Ability	Business situational awareness technology	Mobile Internet malicious program protection products, Internet zombie Trojan worm protection products, key information infrastructure protection products, communication network fraud protection products, security awareness and emergency management platform
	Security situational awareness technology	
	Engine judgment technology	
	Data mining technology based on AI	
Integrated management and control technology of "cloud-network-edge-end"	Emergency coordination and disposal technology	It can be applied to mobile Internet malicious program protection products, Internet zombie Trojan worm protection products, IDC security management products, security awareness and emergency management platforms; It can also be applied to customized information management systems in various industries, such as science and technology supervision, car networking, Internet of Things, industrial Internet and so on
	Flow traction technology	
	Bypass blocking technology	
	Intelligent terminal protection technology	

Chapter 8
Postscript

Abstract A fair and orderly business environment is the cornerstone of national development. Today, with the vigorous development of digital economy, the topic we face together is how to grasp the new situation of economic development to create a good governance environment, and to promote the digital transformation of society. With the rapid development of China's digital economy, Chinese government and enterprises have accumulated experience in optimizing the doing-digital-business environment. The environment for the development of the digital economy is constantly improving. China's practices in optimizing business environment are worth learning from other countries or regions in the world, which covers digital foundation, digital order, digital security, digital services and digital talents.

8.1 Summary of China's Doing-Digital-Business Environment Optimization Practice

A fair and orderly business environment is the cornerstone of national development. Today, with the vigorous development of digital economy, the topics we face together are how to grasp the new situation of economic development, create a good governance environment, and promote the digital transformation of society. With the rapid development of China's digital economy, the Chinese government and enterprises have accumulated experience in optimizing the doing-digital-business environment, and the environment for the development of the digital economy is constantly improving. China's practices in optimizing multi-faceted business environment such as digital foundation, digital order, digital security, digital services and digital talents are worth learning from other countries or regions in the world.

X. Li et al., *Development Practice of Digital Business Environment in China*, Applied Economics and Policy Studies,
https://doi.org/10.1007/978-981-16-8527-9_8

8.1.1 *Policy and Regulatory Documents Provide Optimization Guarantee*

On October 22, 2019, the executive meeting of the State Council of China passed the Regulations on Optimizing Doing-Business Environment. Beijing, Shanghai, Liaoning, Hebei, Shaanxi, Heilongjiang, Jilin, Shanxi, Guangxi, Changsha and Shangqiu successively issued local laws and regulations on doing-business environment, which further standardized and institutionalized the practical achievements and promoted the development of doing-business environment to a higher level from the institutional level. In addition to laws and regulations, Beijing, Shanghai, Guangdong, Shandong, Jiangsu, Zhejiang, Hubei, Jiangxi, Shenzhen, Hangzhou, Shenyang, Sanya and other provinces and cities have issued policy documents and formulated implementation plans, making strategic arrangements and clear division of labor for optimizing the business environment, and providing guarantee for optimizing the doing-business environment. At present, the measures to optimize the doing-business environment vary from place to place. To sum up, they mainly include constructing the evaluation index system and promoting the reform of the commercial system.

(1) Building an assessment index system

Business environment is the embodiment of soft power, and establishing a scientific and reasonable evaluation mechanism can quantify and evaluate business environment. In January 2018, the State Council deployed to set up a doing-business environment evaluation mechanism and further optimize the doing-business environment. According to the deployment of the State Council, the National Development and Reform Commission took the World Bank indicator system as a blueprint, based on Chinese characteristics, and constructed a comprehensive indicator system from three dimensions: measuring the whole life cycle of enterprises, reflecting the attraction of urban investment and reflecting the level of high-quality discovery in cities. They conducted trial evaluation in 22 cities in 2018. In 2019, the doing-business environment assessment was carried out in 40 cities in provinces (autonomous regions and municipalities directly under the Central Government), cities with separate plans, sub-provincial cities, provincial capitals and several prefecture-level cities. In 2020, they conducted business environment assessment in prefecture-level cities and above. According to the practice, some provinces and cities have introduced the doing-business environment assessment index system with local characteristics. The assessment index in Shandong Province mainly includes 17 sub-projects in 6 aspects, such as "enterprise start-up", "access to credit", "real estate registration", "construction permit", "access to electricity" and "tax payment". The Implementation Plan of Doing-Business Environment Assessment in Zhejiang Province (Trial) forms two sets of assessment index systems of districts, cities and counties (cities) from five dimensions: "the whole life cycle of service enterprises", "promoting fair competition", "embodying fair supervision", "optimizing service supply" and "stimulating innovation vitality". At the same time, Zhejiang Province also issued the "Characteristic Index System of Doing-Business Environment in Zhejiang Pilot Free Trade

Zone", and put forward the "3 + 3 + 1" characteristic index system framework of the Pilot Free Trade Zone.

The business environment assessment index system of the World Bank is the most accepted and influential index system related to the doing-business environment in the world at present. But its index is relatively simple, which only focuses on the handling procedures, time and cost of administrative matters in the whole life cycle of enterprises. It enlarges the role of government administration and services, and neglects the requirements of intellectual property protection, market supervision, political and business relations, etc. By comparison, it is found that the business environment index system of the World Bank pays more attention to business efficiency, cost and fairness, while the domestic index systems are more comprehensive and pay attention to regulatory rules, credit construction and high-quality development.

(2) Promoting the reform of the commercial system

The reform of commercial system involves the direct feelings of market subjects in handling affairs. Taking the reform of commercial system as the starting point, it creates a relaxed market access environment, promotes the convenience of the whole process of starting and exiting enterprises, and directly improves the indicators of the doing-business environment.

In terms of relaxing market access, implement the reform of the registered capital registration system, greatly reduce the barriers to entry for enterprises, and stimulate market vitality. We will promote the reform of "separation of licenses" across the country, and solve the problem of no admittance and provide convenience for enterprises to enter the market by directly canceling examination and approval, changing examination and approval to filing, implementing informing commitment and optimizing admittance service. In terms of government service facilitation, the whole process of online office should be implemented to simplify the start-up of enterprises and greatly reduce the registration time for enterprise establishment. Comprehensively, we should promote the application of electronic business licenses, accelerate the reform of enterprise name registration management, and improve social security registration services. Furthermore, we should improve the exit system of market players, implement the reform of simple cancellation registration of enterprises, sort out the matters handled in all aspects of enterprise cancellation, and smooth the channels for enterprise cancellation. In terms of improving the market supervision mechanism, we should fully implement the Negative List of Market Access, adhere to the combination of deregulation, implement the "double random and one open" inspection, and establish and improve the construction of enterprise credit system.

Through various measures of the commercial system reform, the market entry threshold has been lowered and the convenience of registration and cancellation has been greatly improved. The doing-business environment has been optimized, and the number of market entities in the whole country has been growing fast.

8.1.2 Multi-dimensional and Comprehensive Assessment of the Domestic Doing-Digital-Business Environment

With the development of digital economy, the doing-business environment is constantly changing, and the original doing-business environment assessment system is no longer suitable. The Chinese government, enterprises and academic circles began to explore a brand-new index system suitable for doing-digital-business environment assessment, so as to truly understand the reality of the development of digital economy in China. Generally speaking, China's digital economy evaluation has absorbed the advantages and disadvantages of the index system construction in digital economy, innovative human capital and doing-business environment at home and abroad. It has constructed a complete evaluation index system from digital foundation, digital order, digital security, digital service to digital talents.

Digital infrastructure is a new generation of digital infrastructure, which meets the development needs of digital economy, digital society and digital government, and provides data sensing, collection, storage, transmission, calculation, application and other supporting capabilities. Data is filled in every part of digital infrastructure like blood, which is measured by the first-class indicators of network universal service, postal express service, payment means and network guarantee. Digital order mainly measures that whether the current doing-digital-business environment meets the task requirements of "establishing normal market entry, market competition and market transaction order, ensuring fair trade, equal competition and guaranteeing the legitimate rights and interests of operators and consumers". It can be designed into four categories of indicators, namely, market entry and exit order index, transaction order index, competition order index and online network trust guarantee order index. Digital security is an important guarantee for the steady development of digital economy, and its evaluation should build the basic layer index of network security and the application layer index of data open sharing, personal data protection and data cross-border flow operation supervision mechanism. The evaluation of digital service mainly includes three aspects. The first one is the construction of digital government service platform. The second one is the construction of government portal website, and the third is the construction of new government media. Digital talents are the important input energy of the innovation elements of the doing-digital-business environment. The related secondary indicators are developed from the three dimensions of digital talent support, digital innovation activity and digital talent education for measurement.

At present, China has applied the corresponding doing-digital-business environment assessment index system in Beijing, Tianjin, Shanghai and other places to carry out the doing-digital-business environment assessment work. They constantly revise the existing index system in practice.

8.2 Policy Suggestions on Optimizing Doing-Digital-Business Environment

China's digital economy is developing rapidly. To promote the development and construction of China's digital business environment, we should pay attention to the evolution trend of digital economy and digital trade during the 14th Five-Year Plan, so as to promote the development pattern of mutual circulation and mutual promotion of digital economy at home and abroad, to deepen the reform of "distribution suits" in the digital market and to optimize the doing-business environment. We should eliminate the "pain points" and "difficulties" in the production and operation of digital enterprises, and improve the market standardization and international diversification of the doing-digital-business environment.

First, we should strengthen network support. What we need do is to promote the construction of information and communication networks, accelerate the construction of basic network facilities in rural areas, improve the compensation mechanism of universal services in telecommunications services, optimize the upgrading and deployment of new infrastructure such as 5G networks, and promote the optimization and upgrading of operators' broadband services. And then, we should promote the two-way linkage between the supervision information of government agencies and the transportation service information of the express logistics industry, and promote the implementation of the "single window" function, connecting customs law enforcement agencies, logistics services and the upper and lower industrial chains, enabling users to complete independent online inquiry, realizing enterprises to pay various fees online and complete the printing of relevant certificates by themselves. We should promote the optimization and upgrade of online transaction payment system, expand the application scope and application scenarios of online payment and mobile payment, and carry out pilot projects of RMB digitization in areas with relevant circulation conditions. We should explore the market innovation mode in the financial service industry, and further expand the technology performance loan and other businesses in the technology credit products and services, and expand the policy benefits. We should promote the construction of network security system, strengthen the security of e-government information, constantly innovate in network security technology, improve network security products and service systems, and cultivate high-quality and comprehensive network security professionals.

The second is to build an open, fair and orderly market order. We should strengthen the openness and transparency of the market access policy, clean up the unreasonable requirements set by relevant institutions in terms of market access, and clarify the solutions of specific matters, the subjects of responsibilities and rights, and the time limit for handling according to the access rules and regulations. We should construct the feedback mechanism of market subjects and formulate the supervision strategy for the whole process. Based on the principles of openness, fairness and justice, the market rules for trading between the platform and enterprises of all parties are formulated, and the responsibilities and rights of various subjects are clarified, such as the entry and exit mechanism of enterprises, the related guarantee of commodity quality and service quality, the protection of consumers' rights and interests, and the legitimate use of user information. To protect the online business rights and interests of small and micro enterprises, it is strictly forbidden for platform enterprises to abuse their dominant market position and take opportunistic actions, thus damaging the legitimate rights and interests of small and micro enterprises. In order to facilitate the application of intellectual property rights, a special service hall should be established. We should establish the awareness of intellectual property rights, strengthen the protection of knowledge creation, promote the establishment and improvement of intellectual property protection system, strictly punish the infringement and counterfeiting of intellectual property rights, standardize the certification standards of relevant criminal evidence facts, and continuously promote the construction of corresponding protection systems for new formats. At the same time, the pilot work of intellectual property securitization should be vigorously promoted, and efforts should be made to provide enterprises with multi-dimensional, multi-level and comprehensive suggestions on the use of intellectual property rights.

Third, we should strengthen the capacity building of digital government services. We need promote the transformation and development of government services to reach high standards and high convenience. We should implement the comprehensive access of public services to one network, synchronize online and offline standards, and complete all services on one platform. Taking mobile government service as the starting point, we will integrate various resources such as government service system, guide information for handling matters, and convenience window function to promote the micro-service of online government service system. It is suggested that materials such as identification photos, seals and archives should be electronic, so as to enhance the application of electronic identification photos in various party and government organs, enterprises and institutions, and popularize the use of electronic seals in various government affairs. In the multi-channel announcement of the government's "license-free" service catalogue, residents only need to provide corresponding electronic materials when bidding for services in the catalogue. In the process of service, we should establish a "good bad review" system, pay attention to service quality feedback, data reporting speed, follow-up treatment of bad review and other parts, and promote the formation of a closed loop of the "good bad review" system. We should promote the service process of "one form application, one window payment" for start-up enterprises, and the applicants apply and handle all matters related to start-up enterprises at one time through the platform.

The fourth is to cultivate and strengthen the digital talent team. We should constantly strengthen the construction of basic disciplines, promote the connection between industry and teaching, accelerate the training of high-quality and high-level skilled talents, establish and improve the vocational skills learning and training system for practitioners, continuously carry out cutting-edge scientific research and interdisciplinary cooperation, and promote the transformation of scientific and technological research achievements. In terms of talent introduction, we should timely implement the relevant policies for the introduction of high-end talents and the construction of corresponding basic service facilities, and speed up the research and introduction of tax subsidies and incentives for retaining high-knowledge talents at home and abroad and talents in short supply at home and abroad. For skilled talents, we should study a set of index system to evaluate their skill level as soon as possible. By evaluating their professional qualifications, existing professional title information and their own skill level, we can establish a set of promotion sequences of skilled talents that can be compared with those of management and technology, so as to protect the relevant rights and interests of skilled employees and promote the more scientific and diversified development of the evaluation mechanism of skilled talents. We should actively carry out the evaluation pilot work of third-party skilled talents, and encourage employees to use relevant theoretical knowledge and professional skills to complete practical assessment, business appraisal and other appraisal methods to do a good job in evaluation. We should optimize the scientific and technological innovation system, highlight the scientific research project management mode, establish and improve the scientific and technological ethics governance system and scientific and technological evaluation system, build an open innovation pattern, promote the innovation mechanism of environmental construction work and social basic research work, and effectively transform scientific and technological research results. We should improve the infrastructure construction of all kinds of innovation and entrepreneurship in society, and reduce the transaction cost of all kinds of innovation and entrepreneurship personnel to obtain information technology support and innovation and entrepreneurship space.

Fifth, we should promote the steady growth of the digital economy market. We should formulate a digital economy development plan suitable for the local industrial base and endowment characteristics, and optimize the leadership work system. We should promote the development of digital industrialization, drive the innovation and development of industries with cutting-edge technologies, focus on building the information and communication industry, and broaden the trading market of e-commerce and digital trade. We should promote the digital transformation of industry, encourage enterprises to "use data to give wisdom", promote the digital transformation of enterprises, innovate business research and development methods, improve productivity, allocate and optimize enterprise management resources. We should make full use of data resources, realize resource exchange between upstream and downstream industries, promote the allocation and docking of resources in all channels and business links, build an enterprise-platform development ecology, and realize the digital industrial ecology of "production service + business model + financial service". We should promote the further expansion of the digital consumer market, and explore new businesses of digital services such as online education, online medical care and online office work.

The manufacturer's authorised representative in the EU is Springer Nature Customer Service Centre GmbH, Europaplatz 3, 69115 Heidelberg, Germany. If you have any concerns regarding our products, please contact ProductSafety@springernature.com

Printed and bound by CPI Group (UK) Ltd, Croydon, CR0 4YY
30/09/2026
02225338-0002